BUILD A WORLD-CLASS CUSTOMER ADVISORY BOARD

How to Create Deeper Relationships and Validate Strategies

IRENE YAM

IY Media
CALIFORNIA

Paperback ISBN: 979-8-9915603-9-9

eBook ISBN: 979-8-9915603-8-2

Cover and interior design: Andy Meaden meadencreative.com

CONTENTS

Foreword   v

Introduction   A CAB Can Be One of the Most Memorable
     Experiences of Your Career   ix

1   What Is a CAB?   1

2   Principles of a World-Class CAB   19

3   Preparing for a World-Class In-Person CAB   35

4   The World-Class In-Person CAB Event Agenda That
     Creates Trust and Human Connection   81

5   Troubleshooting When an In-Person CAB Plan Goes Sideways   115

6   Executing a World-Class Post-CAB Program   131

7   Hosting a World-Class Virtual CAB   157

8   Hosting a World-Class Hybrid CAB   207

Conclusion   A CAB Is All About Human Connection   227

Appendix   World-Class CAB Resources   233

Author's Note   235

Acknowledgments   237

Foreword

Ninety percent of technology start-ups fail.

I spent my career in B2B start-ups, selling highly technical products to mostly large enterprises around the world. I have been part of eleven of them over about thirty-five years, the last twenty or so as the marketing leader (VP or CMO).

Of those eleven:

- three went public (two with multibillion-dollar valuations);
- two were acquired (both in the billion-dollar range);
- four failed outright;
- one muddled along;
- and one is still going strong as I wait to see whether it goes public or gets acquired.

I feel like I've seen what it takes, I've been through my share of failures and successes, and I think I know why a strong customer advisory board program is so critical.

I'm proud to write this foreword for Irene's book on such an important topic.

The reality is that reaching customers, gaining their trust, and explaining the value proposition of an often unknown technology to people who had trouble understanding it is difficult. Whatever industry you're in, whether it's technology, finance, flying cars, or a new energy drink, understanding customers is the most important—and most often overlooked—step.

The world is littered with tens of thousands of failed start-ups. Most of them probably had smart founders, great products (or so they thought), and big dreams. Why do so many fail? In many, many cases it's partly because of a poor understanding of why customers will (or won't) buy their product.

I've known Irene for twenty-five years. In 1999, I was recruited to a start-up called FastForward Networks. Irene was the office manager. FastForward was building technology to allow large-scale broadcasting over the internet. It's hard to believe today, in the age of streaming, but at that time it just didn't work at scale—you could watch low-resolution clips, but if you wanted to broadcast an NFL game to millions of viewers? No way. FastForward was very exciting and was acquired by Inktomi for $1.3 billion. At that time, Inktomi was the primary search engine on the internet, powering Yahoo! and AOL among others. Unfortunately, shortly after that, Google emerged and absolutely steamrolled Inktomi, which imploded.

Before long we both ended up at Riverbed, a start-up that arose from the wreckage of Inktomi. I was running marketing, and after a few years, Riverbed was accelerating toward our IPO; in fact, at that time, it was the second-fastest hardware startup in history after SUN Microsystems. We brought Irene on, first on the events team, then into customer advocacy. She was so driven and hardworking, and more importantly, dedicated to the success of our customers, that her efforts made a huge difference in our success. Riverbed went public in 2006 and was later acquired for $3.6 billion.

Since then, Irene has become an expert in building, running, and benefiting from a strong customer advocacy program, including how to run a great customer advisory board, one of the central pillars of any advocacy plan.

Why are CABs so critical? I think it's self-evident, but here are a few of the critical things a CAB offers:

- **Direct feedback**. One of the hardest things in any company is to get real feedback from real customers and prospects. A well-run CAB that's taken seriously provides an unparalleled opportunity to talk directly with a group of people in a structured way—they know they're there to give feedback. That feedback should influence your product design, the roadmap, the marketing and messaging, and the approach to selling. You'll also learn a lot about your competitors in a way that's hard to do otherwise.

- **Cross-customer interactions**. One of the most important things that happens at a CAB event are unplanned conversations between customers. Maybe you have a large prospect who's on the fence, or whose deal is stalled. Being invited to a CAB and hearing from existing customers might spark their imagination, help them get over an objection, or make them feel better about taking a big risk, especially when your company is smaller and unknown.

- **Thanking customers and acknowledging their expertise**. Customers often have deep wells of expertise and knowledge, and while their participation in a CAB can help your firm, it also gives the customer the opportunity to help others at the meeting, which can be a great experience. It brings the customer onto your team, into the inner brain trust, and that can really help cement their loyalty and enthusiasm.

- **Building credibility**. One of the biggest challenges we faced at all the start-ups I was part of was mitigating risk for your prospects. When no one has heard of you, or even the category you're a part of, it's very challenging to get the deal. A strong CAB exposes prospects and customers to more than just the sales rep or technical team selling to them. Meeting the executives and technical leadership of a company in a structured way can really help them understand what they're getting into and make them feel more comfortable taking the leap.

As they say, the customer is king. But if your company is not talking to customers regularly in a thoughtful way, you're running a big risk of landing in the 90 percent column, not the 10 percent who succeed. The proven strategies and priceless advice in this book show you how to execute a CAB strategy that will help build your brand, elevate your business, and stay competitive. Irene's advice, honed from years of experience running successful CABs, will guide you to building a great CAB and a strong company.

—**Alan Saldich**
Three-time CMO, Retired

Introduction
A CAB CAN BE ONE OF THE MOST MEMORABLE EXPERIENCES OF YOUR CAREER

The secret to success in business and life is creating meaningful human connections. There is no better example of the pivotal role relationships play than the customer advisory board (CAB), a group of handpicked customers who provide feedback and advice on products and strategy to a company's executive team. I believe hosting a CAB can be one of the most memorable experiences in your career.

I first learned about the importance of human connections while growing up in San Francisco's Chinatown. I'm a first-generation Chinese American (and also part Japanese). My family immigrated to the United States so my father could reinvent himself. My dad spoke English, Japanese, and Chinese, and he was often called to moderate and translate business meetings. I observed him at these meetings, how he listened to and respected all points of view. My fondest memories are of watching him help Chinese shopkeepers find solutions in their dealings with community activists and local politicians. This experience had a profound impact on me.

I found my calling when I helped put together the first CAB for Riverbed Technology, a San Francisco–based technology company in the network space. We worked hard to create CAB meetings that would foster active engagement, respectful discussions, and useful feedback—the same type of environment my father had established in those Chinatown meetings. Customers were given an opportunity to share their opinions and suggestions, and company executives took the time to listen, understand, and connect with their customers. Thanks in part to the CAB, Riverbed became a wildly successful public company with customer advocates around the world.

Is This Book for You?

If you are a CAB manager interested in hosting more engaging and effective CAB meetings, you've picked up the right book. But this book is also for executives who often don't fully understand the purpose and potential of a CAB meeting. In my experience, many executives think a CAB meeting is a sales event or simply a way to meet customers, but they can be much more. This book explains what goes on at a CAB meeting and—whether you're a founder, a chief officer, or a general manager—will help you understand your role; spell out what to expect before, during, and after your event; and reveal what you can achieve with a CAB.

Additionally, this book is for product managers and product marketers who aspire to become leaders. If you've set your sights on being a business leader, this book can help get you a seat on the CAB.

Why World-Class CABs?

Have you heard that your customers are not happy and that renewals have fallen off? Have you heard rumblings from customers about the decline of your service, but you're not sure what needs to be fixed? Or do you have the opposite problem: You are growing, and you want your customers to give you advice on your strategy? Or maybe you have a new product that could be way off base, but your gut and market research tell you it will be successful? A CAB, comprised of six to ten key customers, can help you find out what's really going on and get to the root of the issue.

At CAB meetings, company executives can not only listen to CAB members' advice, they can develop unique relationships with their most innovative and/or largest customers. Typically, the CAB meets in person over one to two days. The agenda is developed to compel deep discussions about strategies, customer experiences, areas for improvement, product or service roadmaps, and broader issues, such as the economy or the challenges of a hybrid workforce. To help company executives make informed decisions, the CAB will offer qualitative data to augment any quantitative data already being used to run the business.

Customers are willing to advise, but they also come with their own agendas. They may want to speak one-on-one with an executive or network with peers who have deployed specific features of your product to get their feedback.

CAB meetings are successful when customers come together to collaborate and provide insights into their businesses and industries. These are some important characteristics of a successful CAB meeting:

- Trust is formed between customers and executives. It is a foundational step in fostering human connections and creating a willingness to help one another.

- Customers advise on strategy and competition. They provide meaningful feedback, including insights on competitors to help keep competition away. To help facilitate this, company executives should tell the CAB members why they were specifically selected to participate from among the competition.

- Customers and executives continue to connect one-on-one, both online and at in-person events. They forge a respectful business partnership where they can advise and confide in one another.

What sets a merely successful CAB apart from a "world-class" CAB is attention to details that promote relationship and trust building and add maximum value for both the customers and executives. By following my five principles of a world-class CAB (which we'll get to later), you'll be well on your way to hosting a rewarding and profitable CAB.

Why Me?

I have been extremely fortunate over my twenty-four-year (and counting!) career to have led a diverse collection of world-class CAB programs for several companies at different stages of growth, including Riverbed, Joyent, EMC, and RingCentral. I know what it takes to run a successful CAB tailored to the unique needs of a sponsor company (including pre- and post-IPO) and the evolving challenges of today's work environment.

I know the value of putting the customer first. At Riverbed, I had the privilege of supporting their first customer advisory board. That experience had a profound career impact on me and shaped my understanding of the value of the customer relationship. I walked away knowing that if we could spend more time in the field with our customers, we would not only win more customers for our product, we would also build true and long-term customer advocacy and quickly catapult Riverbed's brand to the top of the wide-area network space. My belief has only deepened over time. I have doubled down on putting the customer first and emphasizing it as a core value in every customer program I run.

After several successful years at Riverbed, I was challenged to integrate a newly acquired start-up into our yearly CAB event. Being knowledgeable and flexible were pivotal to the new CAB's success. I had to deal with two company cultures (West and East Coast) that had not yet gelled. There were lots of leaders, lots of requests, and lots of heavy-handed suggestions about how to run the CAB for these two companies. I listened to all the requests, but I was guided by our very first CAB and focused on the customers' experience first. It paid off, and I can say with confidence that putting the customer first has always paid off. If you create an experience where there is respect and trust, customers will truly open up and share their feedback. Company executives will as well. They, too, need a safe space to be vulnerable, open up, and ask the hard questions necessary to get meaningful advice from their customer board members.

Over the next five years at Riverbed, as the company continued to grow internationally and evolve, I tweaked and enhanced the CAB program and built a global customer advocacy team.

I know how to tailor a program to a company's unique—and constantly evolving—needs. At Joyent, I decided a standard CAB would not cut it. I needed a new blueprint, one that would help us focus on our technology strategy by creating a Chief Technology CAB. Led by our own CTO and inviting only CTO customers, we gained their trust. The CTO customers on the board immediately clicked. The trusted customers helped not only the CTO with his strategy but advised us through turbulent times and acted as reference customers. Tailoring a CAB is essential these days. With this book, you'll have a set of tools you can use to confidently build a bespoke executive event that supports your business and stands out from your competitors.

I know how to set the right tone across global markets. At EMC, I was challenged to run a CAB focused only on innovative global enterprise customers around the world. I even received a budget to have a CAB meeting in Australia. EMC's world-class sales reps were eager to nominate their customers, so I not only took their input, but would set up web meetings at 10:00 p.m. or 3:00 a.m. to meet these potential customers over a web conference. It was important for me to meet the customers and set the right tone for the CAB from the very beginning. These CABs not only validated our innovative roadmap plans, but they created advocates who volunteered to be design partners. The true stories of planning global CABs I share throughout the book will help you identify and create the ideal tone for your global and regional CABs.

I know how to get results. For some, CABs can be hard to quantify. Most CAB practitioners will send out a survey. I've always enjoyed picking up the phone after every CAB meeting. I believe every touch is important, and I push for company executives who attend the CAB meeting to reach out to their customers. After running these CABs, I have seen:

- Board customers who previously said no to a product demo go back to their sales rep for a demo.

- CAB customers purchase new products.

- Customers from the CAB offer to support marketing events and take timely calls and visits for initial public offer roadshow meetings.

- Executives and customers develop lifelong friendships.

While hard results are ideal, the insights and tips provided throughout this book will have the priceless effect of transforming your company's culture. A world-class CAB can become a North Star for your executives, giving them the confidence to pursue their strategies. Customer board members become the go-to insiders your executives can confide in with confidence and rely on for real-time answers. Over time, these human connections add up to genuine friendships—and a lifetime of value that cannot be tracked on a spreadsheet.

I know how much the behind-the-scenes work matters. CABs are intensive, and much of the work goes unnoticed. But putting in the strategic effort nourishes your company's customer advocacy programs. When I was recruited to join EMC, a public relations and analyst relations leader, the company was *eight weeks* away from the EMC World conference. To say I hit the ground running is an understatement. But I didn't shy away from time-consuming customer outreach. I filmed a launch video, found the best customers for TV spots and analyst relations meetings, recruited thirty-two customers for speaking sessions, and filmed seventeen customer videos. Connecting to our international customers, regardless of time zone, helped us to pack our EMC World conference with innovative global IT leaders and fueled the company's initiatives. The cherry on top? I received an EMC Gold Award for my accomplishments.

I know how to time strategic alliances. RingCentral had its initial public offering (IPO) and set its strategy to go upmarket and start selling to enterprise customers. I was hired for my pre- and post-IPO company experience to lead and grow their customer advocacy programs. The CAB program was undergoing a shift from its focus on midsize to enterprise customers. I had the privilege of reporting to Anita, a RingCentral leader who had founded the RingCentral CAB program. She advised me on how to best elevate the CAB for the executive team to connect with its newest enterprise customers while giving me the space to do it my way. Consequently, I was recognized for strategically timing the best customer references for analyst relations, for the CAB program, and for fueling sales with customer case studies. I was awarded the Most Valued Person (MVP) in marketing for developing strategic alliances, and within nine months I was promoted to senior director for my ability to grow global customer references for annual analyst reports. My experiences and case studies will illustrate why it is important to have a clear customer strategy before running a CAB and will show you how to identify one. I'll even help you tame that voice in your head that second-guesses your approach.

I know how to identify the most effective content. Just before the pandemic in 2020, I brought my experience to a new hybrid role in the UX department at RingCentral. I was challenged to run their beta program and to grow their newest video platform. Adoption was challenging, since many customers were already using a video conference platform.

As I planned for the upcoming CAB meeting, I gathered extensive feedback from our customers to make sure the content of the CAB meeting presentations spoke to their needs and concerns. I learned a great deal about the unspoken IT challenges of onboarding our customer's users (company employees), especially remote workers. I tailored the CAB content accordingly, and customers felt comfortable sharing their concerns and detailed examples of adoption issues with our company executives. Shaping the CAB content in this way helped company executives see the need to put more investment in onboarding, training, and documentation to support customer growth.

While I knew how to connect with customers, this experience reinforced the need to put the customer first and highlighted its importance when building customer advisory board content. I hope you come away from this book knowing why it's so important to communicate thoughtfully and directly. And learn to appreciate the value of giving customers what they want and what they didn't know they could ask for.

I've drawn on my decades of experience and interviewed dozens of colleagues, customers, and executives who worked on CABs and took their CAB responsibilities to heart. Speaking with them has reinforced my belief that CABs are essential for bringing together the key players in business and are needed more than ever to help build relationships and trust in these times of war, inflation, and economic uncertainty around the world.

How This Book Will Help You and Your Business

Based on my twenty-four years of experience running CABs for start-ups and enterprise companies—including business departments and regional CABs—this book will provide you with a framework to create your own CAB strategy to increase customer loyalty, keep competition away, forge long-lasting human connections, and thrive in your career. You'll find practical advice, field-tested planning tools and templates, and case studies.

Here's how the book will unfold.

Chapter 1 will explain exactly what a CAB is and why having one offers a strategic advantage for your company's executives and long-term success. You'll also learn how to measure the benefits of your CAB with CAB key performance indicators (KPIs).

Chapter 2 shares the principles of a world-class CAB and highlights the positive impact they can have on customer experience, company strategies, and post-CAB meeting benefits.

Chapter 3 walks you through every element of preparing for an in-person meeting, including identifying goals, setting expectations, selecting customers and internal company executives, planning the workback, and sticking to the budget.

Chapter 4 shows you how to build a CAB meeting agenda that creates trust and human connection and tailor it to your company's unique needs.

Chapter 5 dives into how to troubleshoot common problems and address difficult situations, such as an upset CAB member.

Chapter 6 focuses on how to use the post-CAB period to foster ongoing conversations with your customer advisers to build business and personal relationships and take your CAB program to the next level. You'll also learn how to create CAB alumni meetings.

In Chapter 7, you'll learn how to hold a virtual CAB meeting that gets high engagement and develops human connections among your executives and the board members.

Chapter 8 covers a hybrid CAB meeting approach—one of the best CAB strategies, in my experience. The case studies and hybrid wisdom I share will help you decide whether running a hybrid CAB meeting is a fit for your company.

In the conclusion, I discuss why I think CABs are about human connection and the kinds of aha moments I think you'll have from being part of a CAB.

The appendix gives you everything you need to produce a CAB meeting—links to all the templates mentioned throughout the book. These templates will save you time and help you stay focused.

1
WHAT IS A CAB?

A CAB (Customer Advisory Board) is a high-level focus group, and a CAB meeting provides company executives and the customers who are on the board an opportunity to get to know one another for a day or two. During this time, they will be able to listen to each other, advise on and criticize current and new strategies, and find solutions to problems. Throughout, I use the term "CAB" to describe both the group and the meeting/event. In this chapter, I'll explain why working together in this way can spark mutually beneficial business connections and even lifelong relationships.

Why Your Company Should Have a CAB

There are several reasons your company would benefit from a CAB. Here are a few:

To validate current efforts. Executives often benefit from CABs by getting validation from their customers about the company's product, service, or strategy.

To build confidence in future strategies. Executives who are unsure of their strategy or vision for the future of the company can receive valuable feedback from a CAB. In some cases, venture capital advisers suggest that CEOs and founders create a CAB to gain that clarity.

To spend more time with customers. Executives often realize that they only meet customers in two situations: when they are called in by the sales team to close a new customer, or when a customer is very unhappy and wants to meet an executive to see what can be done to keep the customer's business. A CAB meeting gives executives the opportunity to interact with customers directly, without the sales team. They learn about their customers and develop a connection with them. Company executives can validate their assumptions with customer board members they trust, and they can be vulnerable about their industry concerns and business views.

To get feedback from customers. This is one of the biggest benefits. Executives gain valuable insight from being in the room for those aha moments when customers show interest and provide their own use case stories on how they would use the company's technology or other products. This feedback may even change the course of the company. Here are company sponsor CAB benefits that I have seen firsthand:

- A start-up ready to go on an IPO tour benefited from customers willing to speak to a global market research firm and advocate for the technology, the company, and its leaders.

- A pre-IPO company that had done extensive research and development (R&D) wanted to launch a new solution. However, every CAB member was against it. This feedback convinced the company not to launch the product. This saved the company tens of millions of dollars and avoided negative press and analyst reviews.

- A post-IPO company that was building out its new teams to support enterprise customers learned that the customer success team, a group of internal experts on products and services, was not given enough training to understand the needs of its enterprise customers. Executives listened and quickly came up with an action plan to ramp up the customer success manager (CSM) team with enterprise training. They asked the head of recruitment to focus on recruiting seasoned enterprise CSMs to quickly support customers.

- During a chief technology officer CAB, CTOs shared constructive feedback on how to make a company's service simpler so they could switch from a competitor's infrastructure-as-a-service (IaaS) to the company's service. They weighed in on software features and tools that the company needed to increase sales.

One of the first executives I worked with on a CAB recognized their value immediately. Josh was the general manager at a global storage company. Nicknamed "the Big Brain," Josh was a vice president by age thirty-five. He started in engineering and product management, and today he's the leader of product strategy for a portfolio of global products that generates over $6 billion in annual subscription revenue across several business units. A gifted leader who appeared relaxed even during difficult discussions, Josh had this to say about the importance of having a CAB:

I look forward to building customer connections at the CAB. Some participants have become my trusted confidants, and there's an unspoken reciprocity after the CAB where we can pick up the phone and help each other out. If I put on my marketing hat, the relationship building we've formed at the CAB builds trust. That trust allows our marketing teams to ask customers for unfiltered feedback on ideas, to get approval for a case study or to speak to the press, or to help us understand competitive strengths and weaknesses.

How Customers Benefit from Joining a CAB

A business or IT leader may spend millions on a company's software, hardware, infrastructure, and services, yet they may never get the chance to meet that company's executives. By joining a vendor company's CAB, customers can influence the vendor's strategy by sharing their expertise. They will also continue to develop their relationships with vendor and peer leadership. Here are some customer advisory board member benefits:

- **Close vendor connections:** Building connections with company executives is a helpful strategy, especially if a product isn't working or there's a service outage. Because they have a seat on the vendor's CAB, CAB members are confident that their issues will be resolved promptly.

- **Direct access to executives:** Members can meet one-on-one to discuss issues and ask vendor executives to look into problems and follow up with solutions.

- **Higher engagement with the vendor:** Customers get access to vendor principals and experts along with complimentary professional services, consulting, and support.

- **Influence on product direction:** Customers can truly influence companies' product strategy.

- **Connections with like-minded peers:** Members can share their experiences and help one another with other vendors.

- **Networking:** CAB members grow their network and ability to connect with other members on other topics after CAB meetings.

- **VIP opportunities:** Members can participate in early betas and get invitations to be flown to speak at industry conferences.

- **Savvier negotiations:** Having a better understanding of the vendor's business helps customers become better negotiators.
- **Discounts:** Members can get future upgrades and lower yearly renewals.

Real Customer Benefit Stories

I first met Adam when we were both starting out in our technology careers. He was a customer, a network engineer at a global natural resources company. Part of my job was to book customers to speak on behalf of my company at one of the largest industry storage conferences. I was asked to focus on IT directors, VPs, or CIOs, but after talking to Adam a few times on the phone, I felt he would be an ideal fit. He was articulate, had extra presence, and understood the tech. My manager trusted me and my decision to choose Adam. He not only spoke at the conference, but he stayed after his talk to answer follow-up questions from many peers and reporters. The following year, Adam became one of our youngest CAB advisers.

Twenty years later, Adam is a VP of technical operations at the largest US auto retailer, with three hundred locations, and has sat on more than forty IT vendor CABs. I asked him for his top reasons for joining a CAB. Adam shared:

Having access to executives and peers to bounce things off is a big perk, and when there is an outage, I have the confidence that my issues will be resolved promptly. Expanding your network through the CAB program does help, especially when I am evaluating other solutions.

More recently, I joined a unified-communications-as-a-service (UCaaS) company just as it was changing its strategy from small-to-midsize businesses to enterprise customers. During this shift, Naveed, an early adopter of UCaaS, who was a CIO at an Ivy League university, spoke openly about his decision to move away from antiquated communications to UCaaS. He agreed to be a public advocate and join our CAB. He didn't join for the honor of being among esteemed colleagues, but to reciprocate and grow together. Naveed shared his experiences and what he valued from sitting on the board:

> When I joined the board, I connected with three other CIOs. Over the next three CAB events, we became inseparable at CABs. Today, we are still friends and still keep in touch. We three CAB members advised on the product roadmap, especially on features for the enterprise market. We were at the nascent edge of technology, and we changed the world. That is foundational, where the company's vision and the customer's goals are aligned to the point where the customer sees the company as the extension of his or her IT staff. That is trust. That is stickiness. That is something so closely intertwined it cannot be separated. It has to be real, authentic, and sincere.

Naveed went on to say more about how he formed close relationships with the UCaaS company's C-suite:

> I was closest to the UCaaS chief operations officer. We built trust during many early conversations in my UCaaS selection process. He and I discussed everything from product to leadership. We became friends because neither was there for their self-interest, and we respected each other.

Over the course of a CAB event, customers gain access to the vendor's backstory, outlook, and strategies, and they get a real sense of who is leading the company.

Vendor and Customer Reciprocity Creates Lifelong Connections

CABs are mutually beneficial to vendor executives and customers, especially because of the human connections established among the participants. If produced well, the CAB event environment allows executives and customers to open up and foster unique relationships based on mutual respect and reciprocity. It lays the groundwork for a lifelong partnership between the customer and vendor that lasts long after the CAB meeting is over.

Here are some examples of customer and executive reciprocation from my experience leading CAB programs:

Trust, Mutual Respect, and Reciprocation

A company filing for an IPO needed vibrant customer stories to share with investment bankers during its IPO road show. We contacted the CAB customers and asked if they would support us. Every CAB customer we asked was willing, and a few of them attended the investment meetings in person.

Customers' Willingness to Be Public Advocates

A software as a service (SaaS) company's executive team wanted to make last-minute changes to the corporate positioning at an annual user conference. Ten days before the conference, they asked my team to film a customer video to promote the new positioning. This would be a challenge because only a small percentage of customers were using solutions linked to this new positioning. Luckily, we had asked one of our CAB customers to describe their use case at a previous CAB, so I reached out to them. The CAB customer made calls to his executive team for support. The customer board member gave us access to his building, staff, and IT team to pull off an on-site video shoot within seventy-two hours. Without the support of the CAB board member and his executive team, we never would have been able to turn around the film so quickly.

Industry and Regional Thought Leadership

At a CAB event focused on financial services in Australia, I flew in five product experts and invited regional executives to attend. After the product leader discussed the upcoming roadmap, a banking board member asked if our roadmap considered the upcoming regulatory compliance. That one question changed the CAB meeting's entire agenda. The head of product sincerely replied, "No, please share with us the new regulatory changes." After a twenty-minute deep dive into the compliance details, the CAB took a much-needed break.

When the CAB got back together, the executives asked the entire board if they could focus more on compliance, and the board agreed. The Australian CAB members were so generous that after the CAB they offered to have ongoing meetings with the teams to provide regular feedback.

Later, the executives learned that the Australian CAB members wanted to be design partners on future features in order to stay competitive in the global market. By becoming early adopters, the Australian CAB members hoped to gain an edge and win more business.

The ongoing CAB meetings and testing helped the company not only grow its business in Australia, but throughout the Asia-Pacific region. The board members volunteered to fly to Japan, Korea, Taiwan, Singapore, Malaysia, Thailand, Vietnam, and Hong Kong to speak at field events. Thanks to their insights on financial regulatory compliance, the company made a big impact in the Asia-Pacific market.

The Australian CAB outcome exceeded our expectations. The CAB customers helped us understand the challenges they faced, and together we developed a camaraderie that helped all of our businesses thrive.

A CEO Contacting CAB Customers About a Latin America Expansion

A company had recently celebrated its IPO, and it was time for the yearly CAB event. The CEO asked me to invite CAB customers with a Latin American regional office. Before creating the CAB agenda, I asked the CEO if he wanted a session just for the Latin American market expansion. He said it wasn't needed. When the VP of marketing, the CAB executive sponsor, and I presented the CAB program for the CEO's final sign-off, he asked to sit next to a multinational bank customer during the board meeting and next to a natural resources customer for lunch. Both of these customers had three or more regional offices in Latin America. After the CAB meeting, the CEO asked for the contact information of these customers, and his executive assistant arranged a follow-up call with them. Two weeks later, the senior vice president of sales hired a general manager of Latin America, and they focused on expanding into Brazil and Mexico. Over time, the CEO's relationships with the two CAB members continued to flourish, and at the CEO's request, the two board members put him in touch with their regional office IT managers in São Paulo and Mexico City.

Within a year, the CEO flew down to São Paulo and Mexico City for the opening of the new Brazil and Mexico offices. When the CEO was touring each city, he asked to have a virtual meeting with the board member, who was back in the United States, and the CAB customer's regional office IT manager. During these meetings, the CEO asked the regional IT managers if they would help support the GM in local field events as guest speakers to discuss how they used the company's products. The regional IT managers didn't mind, especially since they had forged an in-person connection with the CEO and GM. The relationships the CEO developed with the CAB members, initiated at the CAB event, helped boost the company's growth in the new Brazilian and Mexican markets.

Measuring Your CAB Benefits with Key Performance Indicators (KPIs)

You can reap numerous benefits from CABs, and it is important to be able to measure these benefits with hard and soft key performance indicators. KPIs are measurable targets to help you and your programs track whether your CABs are meeting their goals or desired objectives.

With CABs, you'll quickly see soft benefits, such as board members agreeing to test a new product and/or expressing a willingness to talk to analysts. But that is not to say that CAB meetings don't generate hard benefits. You will capture hard metrics, but that is after the CAB event, when the customer purchases new and/or additional products and services.

Alan, an experienced business-to-business (B2B) chief marketing officer with several pre- and post-IPO experiences, has this to say about metrics:

CAB metrics aren't cut-and-dried like sales numbers, but they can be indicators of how customers view your company, and sometimes they really help you change direction in important ways. You can't say that a CAB program will result in X dollars in Y months. But CABs give executives confidential time with their most influential customers to deepen their relationships, and that can drive future business. Sometimes what you hear at a CAB can be negative but nonetheless helps you focus.

During one session, we unveiled a future product idea, and the unanimous feedback was that because of security concerns, they would not buy the product even though technically it had incredible functionality. Although that wasn't the outcome we wanted, by getting early feedback from our most important customers, we ended up saving millions of dollars on research and development and focused on our core products.

CAB Hard KPIs

Three internal systems are connected to a CAB's hard metrics: a net promoter score (NPS) platform, your company's customer relationship management (CRM) platform, and customer advocacy technology.

NPS surveys ask customers, on a scale of 0 to 10, "How likely are you to recommend Company X to a friend or colleague?" This metric is important because it provides a measurement of growth and overall customer satisfaction. The customer NPS surveys are stored on the platform to help analyze trends and provide customer data that can by filtered by size, personas, and industries.

With CRM systems, you can track whether the customer purchases more products or services after the CAB meeting. Often, CAB members will buy more products because of the trust that has developed with the company executives. The CRM insights will be the most significant data to measure hard KPIs.

Customer advocacy technology is managed by one or more customer advocate members, who focus on tracking how many times a customer supports a vendor's sales reference or marketing activity. For example, customer advocate members would use the technology to note whether a CAB customer who had previously declined to speak at industry conferences about their case study is willing to support the requests after the CAB meeting, because of the connections they made with vendor leaders. Post-CAB meeting, customers often want to reciprocate by offering to take more sales reference calls and attending networking events to share their experiences with the company.

Figure 1: Customer Data That Lives Across Three Systems

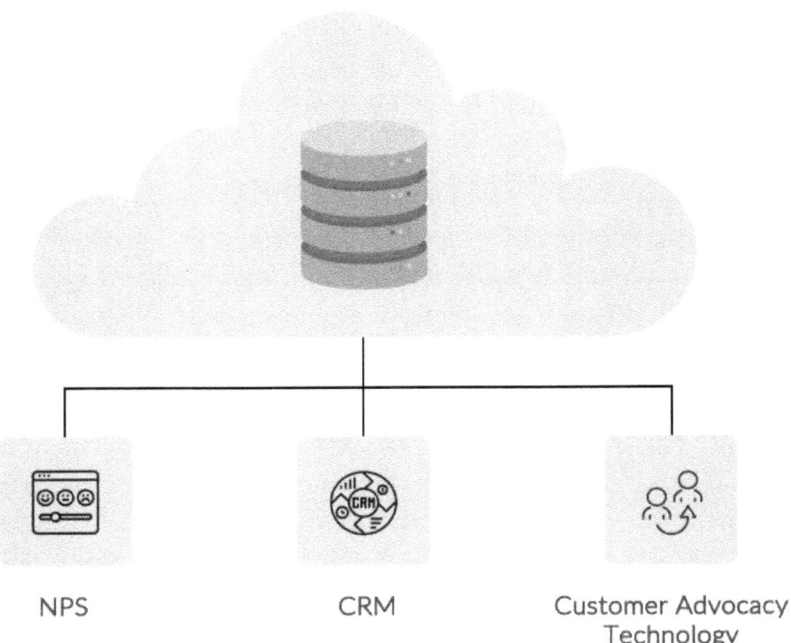

NPS   CRM   Customer Advocacy
                                              Technology

Examples of hard KPIs:

- An increase in the customer satisfaction rating

    o Measure the net promoter score (NPS) customer surveys before and after the CAB event.

- An increase in the customer lifetime value (used mostly by customer marketing teams)

    o Post-CAB event, customers will ask the sales team for a proof of concept (POC) or trial of products or services, because they have been reassured by their board peers' candid feedback on how well the products or services work. These peer interactions during the CAB have a positive impact. CAB customers typically will increase their average customer lifespan as a result of sitting on the board. When purchasing new products and services, their average purchase value is higher than the general average. And most CAB customers increase their spending and will purchase new products.

- Accelerated sales (used by sales operations teams)

  o Measure if a CAB event fast-tracks a sale by comparing it to the average number of days it takes to close a sales opportunity.

  o Measure and highlight new sales opportunities after a CAB event.

  o After a CAB meeting, pull a monthly report to determine whether CAB customers are now trialing other products and services.

  o Continue tracking CAB members' buying behavior. Most CAB customers will go back to their sales representative asking for a POC for a product that they previously said no to, after learning from a CAB peer that the product or service works as marketed.

At a network appliance company, I added an additional CAB to the existing CAB because the company acquired a start-up. Three months after the two CAB events, 50 percent of the existing CAB customers purchased the other CAB's solutions. The hard KPI was due to merging the two CABs morning agendas to bring cohesiveness between both boards and allow ample time for networking, which led to natural cross-selling.

Dennis, who led global sales at the network appliance company and built and scaled the team from zero to $800M in eight years, had interesting insights to share on CAB hard KPIs. I thought he would focus on faster sales velocity during the CAB program. Instead, Dennis was adamant that only innovative customers should be invited to a CAB, not just customers with global brand recognition.

Internally, executives will talk about what kind of CAB they want to have. Most of my colleagues want to hear from innovative customers. They also want to invite the top accounts, but the innovative customers validate our company's strategy, suggest where we should invest in our research and development, and give us insights into our competition.

Inviting the biggest accounts helps us tactically scale operations and retain customers. The CAB members provide a 180-degree view of their experiences from onboarding to upgrading. Their advice is genuine, and customers don't seem as guarded in a board setting.

He went on to describe some distinctive aha moments in a CAB that can impact hard KPIs:

I guess this is the engineer in me, but the biggest value for me is when I see CAB customers light up when they understand our strategy behind the roadmap, and how it can impact their business. Hearing how customers would apply features and having other board members share their use cases is that moment for me. When customers get excited about our roadmap, I've noticed that the same CAB customers either fast-track their purchase and/or are willing to do a proof of concept of a product they said no to months ago.

NPS Customer Surveys

In all companies, the net promoter score (NPS) is considered the metric to predict customer growth. CABs make an impact by increasing company NPS scores and helping to move sales opportunities along.

Most executives who sponsor CABs tend to justify the meetings as a sales event. However, I believe the increase in sales should come organically. The CAB provides collaboration and a chance for customers to have one-on-one time with company executives. These are the actions that will eventually drive sales. During the CAB meeting, board members exchange casual product testimonials with peers, which facilitates trust between board members.

Regarding a CAB and its NPS influence, when board members are asked after the CAB event how likely they are to recommend the product or service, they typically tend to provide a high rating of 9 or 10. These CAB members have become customer advocates in their industries. They blaze the trail for their peers to follow. The CAB customers' stories encourage more customers to become public promoters. That's how word of mouth spreads. Customers become proud to share they are customers and company advisers. This naturally leads to their willingness to take peer-to-peer reference calls and write reviews on third-party analyst sites.

CRM: Customer Lifetime Value (CLV) and Sales Opportunities Data

A company's CRM platform is where the customer lifetime value (CLV) and sales opportunities data can be found for every customer. After a CAB, board members are likely more receptive to new product offerings, which increases the CLV. They will often become early adopters and select your solution over a competitor's as a result of the relationships forged at the CAB event.

Examples of sales opportunities data include the following:

- The opportunities-to-sales conversion rate

- Which sales opportunity stages are skipped after a CAB event

- The number of products and services purchased after a CAB event

- The number of early adopters of products and services after a CAB event

After a CAB meeting, sales stages are often skipped because customers leave with newly formed relationships with board peers and the executive team. For example, customers may be in sales negotiations prior to the CAB. During the event, the CEO and CAB members may engage in one-on-one conversations or discuss their experiences with CAB peers. These moments effectively move them forward in the sales process.

NPS and CLV data can be tricky for CAB leads to measure because they are not always given direct access to the information. They often need to partner with the customer experience and marketing teams to get access to their systems and reports.

CAB Lead Pro Tip: Ask your CAB sales executive to ask a colleague in the sales operations team to pull a custom report on each customer board member before the CAB event.

After the CAB, pull this report monthly to check each customer's account. Within three months, you will see how the CAB has affected your sales. (You'll need to have a control group to measure accurately.)

Customer Advocacy: Customers' Willingness to Take Private, Peer-to-Peer Reference Sales Calls

CAB customers will often take an additional ten to twenty private reference calls and advise peers throughout the year compared to a non-CAB reference customer who may take only three to five reference calls a year. Customer reference reports are easy to pull, as the data is accessible in the customer advocacy technology that is used to track customer reference sales calls, which is connected to the CRM.

CAB Soft KPIs

All the chief marketing officers, vice presidents, and general managers of business units I've interviewed have mentioned how having a CAB builds trust between the customer and company. They open up opportunities for co-branding initiatives and industry conference partnerships. Often after a CAB event, board members will be open to asking their leadership to speak to the press, present at a conference, or film a video for the CAB sponsor.

Examples of soft KPIs include the following:

- Development of trust, mutual respect, and reciprocation

- Customers' willingness to be public advocates and contributors to videos, press releases, speaking engagements, case studies, and product reviews

- Industry and regional thought leadership creation

    o Deeper understanding of customer industries, including risks and growth areas

    o Regional views and conventional buying habits

Chapter 1 covered the following:

A CAB is a high-level focus group and meeting that gives customers and company executives an opportunity to get to know each other.

There are several benefits that your company can gain from a CAB, including validating current efforts, building confidence in future strategies, spending more time with customers, and getting feedback.

- Your customers can also benefit from joining your CAB, where they can make close vendor and peer connections, get direct access to executives, influence product direction, and negotiate discounts.

- A CAB can act as a catalyst for creating valuable long-term relationships between your company and your customers.

- How to measure what you achieved from your CAB using hard and soft KPIs.

The next chapter will cover the five principles that are foundational to forming a world-class CAB.

2
PRINCIPLES OF A
WORLD-CLASS CAB

I've used a popular buzzword to describe the type of CAB I advocate: world-class. But what does that word mean? Let's first check the Merriam-Webster dictionary. Its definition of world-class is: *being of the highest caliber in the world.*

You might think that a world-class CAB event is held at a luxury, five-star venue on a budget of $200,000 to $300,000. The company would fly their CAB customers to Napa for one to three days, rent private black cars, host wine tastings, and serve four-course meals. That's what I would describe as an expensive CAB event. In my experience, a world-class CAB meeting can happen on any budget; it's the time and thought that goes into planning it that make it world-class.

Having a CAB with big brand customers and/or a big budget doesn't necessarily mean that you'll have a world-class CAB. An important part of a world-class CAB event is setting clear expectations with your executives and customers on the board. It also involves providing value for customers and executives, earning customers' respect and trust, and making every minute of the CAB meeting count. Above all, details matter. To make it easy for you to host your own world-class CAB event, here are the components, distilled into five principles:

1. Be respectful of time.

2. Be thoughtful and empathetic.

3. Prepare.

4. Follow the CAB mission statement.

5. Take action and follow up.

The way my dad facilitated the meetings in Chinatown helped me identify these principles. As a kid, I didn't know much about what was going on, but I would sit in the back of the meeting room and watch. I noticed that the energy and mood in the room improved when the snacks were better, like fresh dumplings or delicate egg tarts. And even though the meeting may have officially ended, people would stick around to hang out, talk, laugh, and enjoy the treats. Snacks may seem like a small thing, but just like at those community meetings, paying attention to the details can make all the difference, and it's the sum of the details that makes a CAB world-class.

In this chapter, I'll explain each of the five world-class CAB principles in detail and show you how to apply them to run your own world-class CAB. I have strong feelings about in-person CAB meetings. It's so much easier and more effective to connect with customers and explain new concepts and strategies in person than over a video conference call. In person, people can read your body language and, without sounding too woo-woo, customers can feel the energy you exude. But whether you decide to host an in-person, virtual, or hybrid CAB (I'll cover virtual and hybrid CAB events in chapters 7 and 8), your first planning step will be to commit to following my world-class CAB principles.

Committing to World-Class CAB Principles

Though the following recommendations are directed to the CAB lead, these principles should be followed by everyone who is a part of the CAB, including customers. These principles will help you develop your own world-class CAB.

> **CAB Lead Pro Tip:** Set expectations around your CAB
>
> If you need to scale down your budget, be open with the members of the board and executive team. Reassure them that even though you will be operating with a smaller budget, you are committed to creating a CAB packed with experiences to facilitate connections.

1. Be Respectful of Time

Time is coveted by both your board customers and your executive leadership. When planning your in-person CAB event, you'll be asking your executives and customers, who already have very demanding schedules, to travel and be away from family. To make the most of everyone's time, be sure to do the following:

- Plan and polish the CAB meeting agenda. The CAB experience must run with ease, but attention to detail and ensuring time for discussions is essential for a world-class CAB.

- Arrange for the best speakers and facilitators to attend the event.

- Vet the speakers' presentations to make sure they have been tailored to the CAB meeting and have not simply been plucked from well-worn sales pitches. Never make the CAB presentation a sales pitch.

- Fill the day by asking your executives to provide an insider's view of the company. Encourage executives to weigh in with their views and be sincere when asking customers and board members to elaborate rather than going into attack mode.

- Allow time for customers and executives to interact. Customer board members should feel free to open up and share and walk away from the CAB feeling heard and respected.

2. Be Thoughtful and Empathetic

Lead with thoughtfulness and empathy in the planning, communication, and action stages. Customer board members are more likely to reciprocate partnerships when your company treats them well and makes it easy for them to take on new responsibilities and actively participate. Being thoughtful and empathetic involves the following:

- Integrate multiple learning styles and approaches to get your message across, such as smaller breakout meetings, printouts, hands-on demonstrations, and video presentations.

- Find ways to help customer board members participate more easily and fit the role of being an adviser into their already busy life. For instance, the board members may not know each other, and you can't expect them to collaborate by just putting them in a room together. Prior to the CAB meeting, the CAB lead should help them connect by creating a CAB biography handout or asking everyone to make a short introduction video to be shared ahead of time.

- Assure customer board members that the CAB meeting will be a safe environment for constructive discussion and criticism and ask each customer board member to be thoughtful and empathetic with the content that executives will be sharing.

- Be observant. There will be customers who take longer to warm up and find their confidence to speak up. Some will be shy with peers. Check in on the quiet customers during the CAB event. Ask them if they need anything. Often, they may have one burning question that's easy to ask an executive to bring up. You can also offer the customer one-on-one time with an executive.

3. Prepare

Everyone involved in the CAB should prepare: the CAB lead, executives, and customer board members. Too often, CAB participants don't adequately prepare for the meeting, and a lack of preparation can mean the difference between a world-class CAB event and a "just okay" one.

For the CAB lead, preparing for the event means coaching participants, arranging practice sessions, sending reminders about important deadlines and meetings, checking (and double-checking) every detail of the day—from the seating and lighting arrangements to the food and transportation—and taking in feedback during each stage of the planning process to fine-tune the CAB experience.

It can be challenging to convince executives of the need to prepare for a CAB meeting. Internal leaders are often overconfident or think they can wing it because they'll be speaking to a small group of customers. Many CAB meeting internal speakers may never have presented in a CAB format. The CAB lead should be prepared to coach the executives who will be speaking so they can deliver a strong and effective presentation. This includes reminding and helping internal leaders to create succinct presentations and preparing them to anticipate questions and concerns from customer board members.

Customer board members should expect to prepare as well. The CAB lead should ask customers to come ready to share their company's perspective on the host company's products and/or services and remind them that they may find it useful to prepare by reaching out to their direct reports and/or super users.

The preparation phase can be the most stressful, especially for the CAB lead. It's challenging to keep reminding speakers, especially executives, to be prepared for a dry run or to finalize their slides a few days before the event so the design team can review them for final adjustments. Remind your speakers of the importance of the team collectively presenting itself well in front of the CAB and how their presentations are crucial to building the company's brand and instilling trust with customers.

4. Follow the CAB Mission Statement

Each CAB meeting should have a mission statement, shared with all participants, identifying what the C-suite executives would like to learn from CAB customers. The CAB mission statement sets the tone for the meeting and establishes its parameters so board members know what to expect—and know this isn't a vendor sales meeting. If there is no mission statement, there is no accountability or way to bring the board back to focusing on what is important to achieve during the CAB meeting. Everyone involved in the CAB meeting should strive to stay within the scope of the mission statement, but it's especially important for the CAB lead to maintain alignment with it at every stage of planning and execution. For more on mission statements, see page 40.

5. Take Action and Follow Up

Taking agreed-upon next steps and following up as necessary should be a priority for all CAB meeting participants, but it is the CAB lead's responsibility to make sure it happens. This can start in the planning stage by reminding company executives and speakers of their responsibility to follow up as needed. During all CAB meeting sessions (large group and one-on-ones), a notetaker should be present to record all customer questions so that an executive can be assigned to provide the answer or more information. After a CAB event, a best practice is to bring all the company CAB attendees together to assign and confirm who will take certain action items and follow up with customers. This will often result in a web meeting to follow up with the entire board.

These world-class CAB principles establish a foundation for your internal team and your customers. CABs are an investment not just to achieve your goals, but much more. The relationships made with your customers will increase customer loyalty. The CAB will also help fuel success and build a positive company culture of empathy and respect with executives empowered to go out of their way to make customers happy.

Putting the Principles into Practice

Simon the Pissed-Off Customer

Simon (name changed to protect his privacy) ran IT for a global retail company, and he was a customer participant at a very large CAB meeting I was running. When he entered the kickoff happy hour, he seemed angry. Others noticed it, and he almost parted the room with his energy.

Since I was the organizer, I approached Simon to check in. I was nervous. I asked him if I could get him a cocktail, showed him where the food was, and said I would meet him there with his cocktail. We made very little small talk. He ate, drank, and then asked for the head of product. I said, "Okay. Let me see if I can get you and our head of product a place to talk." I was worried. He seemed really upset and looked like he was about to blow up. I thought I could relax him with some chitchat, food, and drink, but that didn't seem to work.

I went to Mike, our head of product, and told him how upset this customer was. Mike understood and said, "Let's talk on the veranda facing the ocean." I brought Simon over. Throughout the night, all I could do was check in from afar. Simon had a lot to say. After he stomped off, I went over to Mike to find out what transpired. "He's upset, and he needed someone to hear him out," Mike said. I thanked Mike profusely for taking one for the team.

Simon was brooding when I checked in with him later that night. He answered my questions only with a yes, a no, or a nod. He seemed calmer, but I felt it best to give the man space. I texted Jimmy, the customer success manager (CSM) of the account the next morning, and he responded, "Oh, he's like that. He can be this way. That's normal." Even with the CSM's reassurance, I worried I hadn't done a good enough job to help this customer.

To my surprise, when the bulk of the CAB meetings were done the next evening, Simon walked over and thanked me. He said, "That was a lot of work that you put into the CAB. I saw the details. That's not easy. You made it easier for me to connect with executives. I'm glad that I'm on the board." I smiled because I felt he meant it. What a turnaround; just over twenty-four hours ago he had been stomping around the room, but now Simon seemed happy to be there.

The company had spent a lot of money on this CAB, but I don't think it would have mattered to Simon. Access and time was what Simon wanted: space to connect and time to have one-on-one meetings with our executives. Once he accomplished his goals, he was more open to relaxing that night and was very engaged the next day. These five world-class CAB principles made the difference:

1. **Respecting his time** by giving him an opportunity to fulfill his goals.

2. **Being thoughtful and empathetic** by reaching out to him, but giving him space, listening to his needs and taking them seriously, and doing our best to meet them in a timely manner.

3. **Preparing** by way of a happy hour before sitting down for long meetings, to break the ice, network, and begin to build rapport with board members.

4. **Following the CAB mission statement**, which in this case was to ask the board how the company can best offer enterprise solutions, and whether they would they act as early design partners to help the company develop their future research and development strategies.

5. **Taking action** at the CAB meeting by connecting him with relevant resources and following up afterward to make sure he was satisfied.

Case Study: *An Australian CAB Helped Spin Off a Network and Volunteered to Be Early Product Design Partners*

In chapter 1, I described the benefits a leading global storage company experienced after having a CAB event focused on financial services in Australia, particularly business growth in Australia and throughout the Asia-Pacific region. This CAB event is an excellent example of the power of the five principles at work, so here are more details to illustrate this.

The company's Australian customers were known to be early adopters and open to testing new solutions. They had a very strong Australian general manager and a team of sales executives who had great relationships with their accounts. The GM was able to recruit an eclectic list of potential CAB attendees: he could handpick customer contacts from the top financial services firms, government agencies, and transportation companies.

On average, these customers spent $40 million-plus annually on storage, so the case for giving them a voice and establishing a CAB in Australia was clear. The US company's executives and their EMEA product management leaders flew in to support the CAB. Since many of us didn't have relationships with these customers, we invited the company's strongest sales engineer, who happens to be an Australian living in California, to support the CAB. We had a great kickoff dinner overlooking Sydney Harbour and held our meetings in a recently renovated historic five-star hotel.

After the company overview, we had our first guest speaker, a CAB customer who was a storage architect from the Australian postal service. I had planned this carefully. The architect had been hired to transform the agency's IT infrastructure and bring it into the digital age. His success was energizing and inspiring. At the preparation stage, I helped co-create his slide presentation, and we did a few trial runs over video conference. This ensured that he was well prepared. When the architect presented and shared how he had left his lucrative job in the private sector to serve his country by transforming this government agency system, you could feel the excitement and energy in the room. Afterward, many shared that it was the most uplifting peer story they had heard in a while. The customer felt like a rock star and immediately gained a roomful of new friends.

Most of the other presentations were given by product management experts. The director of product marketing had taken ownership of the slides, but we had conducted several dry runs (over video conference) with all the participating product management experts to ensure they were prepared. At first, it was a little quiet when a presentation concluded, with customers keeping to themselves, but our Australian-born sales engineer sprang into action. As he spoke and facilitated, customers opened up and the discussion got going.

After the CAB event, the GM and the sales executives gave us heaps of positive feedback. Many CAB customers wanted to help design future product strategy to ensure the solutions were compliant with regulatory and risk policies. This was a win.

Here's what Tamir, the product leader, had to say:

After the CAB, we established an early beta access program because of the rapport between the customers and our product leaders. The beta feedback gave us deeper insights on what was important to our customers, how to position the product, and how to sell into the Asia-Pacific market. That year, our sales team achieved record-level sales in the region. Our positioning worked, but what I took away was how to connect with the customers at the CAB and be open to pivot off their ideas, to keep asking questions to flush out the ideas. Although CABs are a lot of work for our product and our executives, they are events I'll always volunteer to lead. To me it was eye-opening to see the impact in the following quarters on the business and how we could utilize the newly formed connections to better build and market the product in Asia-Pacific.

The CAB event had also deepened connections among the members and triggered many follow-up conversations, partnerships, and future knowledge sharing. They talked about helping one another on new projects and setting up visits to their offices in downtown Sydney.

The CAB event provided clear value to all participants. Not only did we help develop a new network among the customers, but customers wanted to reciprocate by being advisers during our product design planning to save us from making costly mistakes.

Hosting this CAB proved how a board meeting is much more than just a way of validating strategies and product or service roadmaps. A world-class CAB event brings people together, forges connections, and builds lasting relationships founded on trust among customers and between customers and the company.

One of my mentors, Anita, is an experienced executive, and she shared her approach to hosting a world-class CAB meeting:

Take the time to convince those who will be attending the CAB that this isn't just a one-time event to extract information. A CAB represents a genuine commitment to forging a strong partnership with your customers. Understanding their business, professional challenges, and product feedback is important, but genuinely connecting with them as individuals holds even greater importance. Be authentic and the long-term partnership will emerge.

The true value of the CAB is what happens among its members in the long term. The five world-class CAB principles made the difference at the event we hosted in Australia:

1. **Being respectful** of time by listening, opening up the CAB, and giving the board members the floor to share their pain and what solutions they wanted.

2. **Being thoughtful and empathetic** by thanking our board for taking the initiative and giving our executives more time to build empathy for the unique needs of the Australian customers.

3. **Being prepared** to put aside our roadmap and to listen to our board members. We were able to spend time with our customers on the top crucial roadmap questions.

4. **Following the CAB mission statement**, which in this case was achieved differently but in a positive manner. The board members helped us accomplish our mission by sharing their challenges.

5. **Taking action and following up afterward.** We gained so much from the board's advice that we ended up having the board volunteer to be design partners. Often one has to coax a customer; here customers wanted to co-design.

Case Study: *A SaaS Company Set Their Sights on the Enterprise Market*

This case study involves a CAB hosted by a SaaS company that had at first sold to small and midsize businesses but now wanted to shift their SaaS offerings to enterprise companies. Their executives were introverted, yet they knew it was important to start building one-on-one relationships with customers because of the way enterprise customers preferred to purchase.

The CAB meeting was a two-day event in Napa, California. Eighty percent of the customers were new enterprise customers who had purchased within the last year. Twenty percent were drawn from the company's existing base of midsize customers and were savvy CAB veterans. Over the past year, our CAB veterans had advised us on how to sell to enterprise customers, so it was no surprise to them when we candidly asked them for help. We wanted these CAB veterans not only to become board members, but to be connectors by facilitating conversations privately and by helping make connections between the executives and the enterprise customers.

My manager, a fast-rising vice president, was instrumental in selecting these customers for the board. By including CAB veterans who had not only served on our company's board before but had also served on other technology boards, she created a pool of natural ambassadors for our company. IT professionals with more than sixteen years of experience, these veterans were also friendly and adept at cold networking.

Kicking Off the CAB

The veteran CAB members were terrific at pulling people into their happy hour discussions. One customer was so good at it that our CEO noticed and made a point of joining his conversation. These interactions set a congenial tone and built camaraderie among customers and executives.

Facilitating Conversations During the Quiet Periods

The senior vice president of product management became our company executive sponsor. The VP took the CAB presentation seriously by weaving in details to solicit deeper discussions on what to build for enterprises. The VP would pause for the customer to speak up, and when no one opened up, a customer veteran tossed an "easy" question back to the VP, asking to go back to a slide for clarification. The pause turned into a lively debate about a proposed feature and how if it was to be turned on, most customers would need to send their administrators to training. It was a great insight, and the chief customer officer in attendance took notes on how to best offer a beta training class for the CAB members.

Even the Reserved Thrived

We knowingly invited some reserved enterprise customers to join our board because our executive team, from mostly smaller and midsize companies, had not spent much time with global customers. These enterprise customers mentioned to their sales engineers that they were early adopters who had resources to test and provide product feedback. We needed customers who would be willing to provide resources to test features and give us timely feedback. Two of the enterprise customers were surprisingly shy and seemed to be smirking, and I couldn't read whether they were interested or dissatisfied. During the first break, I asked our most calm and thoughtful veteran customer if he wouldn't mind going up to the quiet customers when he could to ask what they thought of the CAB. He found out they were just shy and had never been to a CAB meeting. Over lunch, I moved the two shy people into the veteran CAB customer's afternoon breakout session. I knew the shy people needed to feel safer to speak up. I was not wrong. During the breakout session on Support, both enterprise customers had a lot to say about supporting remote offices in Asia. We took note and followed up with them that we would be hiring additional tier 1 support engineers. While that was not why we asked the two reserved customers to attend, it's the quiet customers who often offer excellent feedback.

Even the introverted executive team built formative relationships with the enterprise customers during the CAB. They found their own way of connecting by having one-on-one conversations and collaborating through notes and sketches on napkins and notebooks.

Soon after the CAB meeting, the enterprise customers asked for demos of our lesser-known solutions. Because of the CAB's success, the CEO asked for the CAB program to triple in size and to expand into additional geographic regions.

The five world-class CAB principles helped make this success happen:

1. **Being respectful of time.** Inviting our newest and biggest enterprise customers was a challenge, and we wanted to create a special experience because we knew they had a choice to sit on our board versus other boards. Inviting the veteran board members to act as ambassadors to these customers helped bridge connections between our introverted company executives and new board members.

2. **Being thoughtful and empathetic** by changing our board seating arrangements to help the two reserved board members feel comfortable by being seated next to a veteran board member.

3. **Being prepared** by asking our veteran customer board members for help on facilitating discussions between new board members.

4. **Following the CAB mission statement** by planning more breaks and bringing in new executives to share action plans.

5. **Taking action** and following up afterward with our board members and listening to their advice to ensure we had tier 1 engineers to support our Asia customers.

Create Your Own Definition of a World-Class CAB

World class is something you can define for yourself. The five principles I've identified in this chapter have served me well during my more than two decades of running CABs for nine different technology companies. As I led more CABs, I found that the most successful were the ones that aligned with my principles and the specific company's values. While all the principles contribute to a world-class CAB, when it comes to company executives, it's essential to emphasize how important it is to prepare, prepare, prepare. Be positive when it comes to reminding your speakers to practice their presentations, since a strong CAB presentation is not just about knowing the topic, but about practicing pauses, asking questions, and knowing how to answer tough questions.

Chapter 2 covered the following:

- A world-class CAB doesn't need to be expensive, but it does require time and thoughtfulness to plan it.

- The five principles of a world-class CAB: be respectful of time, be thoughtful and empathetic, prepare, follow the CAB mission statement, and take action and follow up.

- Case studies with examples of how following these principles took these CABs to the world-class level.

In the next chapter, you'll learn how to prepare for an in-person CAB. This will include the roles and responsibilities of your internal CAB team, your company executives, and CAB customers.

3
PREPARING FOR A WORLD-CLASS IN-PERSON CAB

Now that you've committed to having a world-class CAB, let's get to it! In this chapter, you'll learn the key components of planning the board meeting, including selecting the customer board members and the executives, creating the CAB mission statement, and planning the budget. (We'll focus on setting the agenda in chapter 4.) Much of the planning and post-CAB processes for an in-person event can be applied to a virtual or hybrid CAB event.

Identifying Key Customer Advisory Board Internal Roles

Before you do any planning for the CAB, make sure you or your manager have the full support of your CEO. You want the CEO's support for the CAB because many top company resources will be asked to support the board meeting. In some cases, the CEO may be the company executive sponsor of the CAB, but if they are not, you'll want confirmation of their commitment to the CAB.

The following are the key roles you should have on your CAB preparation team and their responsibilities.

Company Executive Sponsor of the CAB

The CEO may take on this role or they may appoint a chief officer to be your company executive sponsor, such as a chief operations officer or chief customer officer. The company executive sponsor elevates the importance of the CAB and aligns the rest of the C-suite leaders, ensuring that the right internal experts are supporting the board meeting.

Your company executive sponsor won't have time to create CAB presentations, but they can help you remove barriers, pass budgets, and review all CAB content. They will need to sign off on the final CAB presentations.

CAB Lead

The CAB lead will direct the entire program and is essential to its success. Their responsibilities include planning, being at the board meeting, following up with customers, and managing the post-CAB executive sponsorship program (more on this program on page 142). This person catches and anticipates CAB issues that need to be solved prior to the live board meeting and troubleshoots issues as they arise at the event.

No matter the size of your company, you should always have one CAB lead who oversees the CAB from the start and is the main point person throughout. Typically, the CAB lead is in customer marketing, customer reference, or customer advocacy. If there's no such manager in your company, ask a vice president of product marketing or someone equivalent to be the CAB lead.

Product Management and Product Marketing Managers (General Managers)

Since CAB presentations can often be technical, product management and product marketing managers are necessary to ensure the CAB meeting messaging and positioning of the company's products and services align with the company executive sponsor's vision.

Your product management manager is in charge of the development of product features. They're also in charge of creating the product or service roadmap for the CAB. They should work closely with the chief product officer or the product leader who will present at the CAB meeting.

The product marketing managers will help review the roadmap presentation and make sure it uses industry terms correctly and includes the right messaging. It's important to create clean, clear, and accurate product messaging, especially during the CAB. Otherwise, the board will end up picking at the confusing message and not focus on giving constructive product feedback.

Design

Your brand and design team or lead will help create all the CAB meeting visuals, including the company CAB brand, logo, and presentation slides. They should also collaborate with product management and/or product marketing to make the CAB roadmap presentation more appealing with illustrations or graphics.

Subject-Matter Experts (Optional)

Subject-matter experts who have presence and can keep customers and executives engaged can help elevate CAB presentations. Having these experts speak—or, even better—co-speak with an executive can be beneficial, especially in situations where an executive isn't an especially engaging speaker.

Legal

Your legal team or lawyer will be responsible for creating a disclaimer for the beginning of the CAB presentation and a mutual nondisclosure agreement (MNDA) for customers to sign. It's always best to ask your customer to sign the CAB MNDA right after you have confirmed they will be joining. Some customers who come from big companies will likely have a clause in their contract or from their own legal team about attending meetings and sharing information, and that can sometimes serve as your CAB MNDA. Always have your counsel review this language and confirm it is acceptable. The CAB lead is responsible for making sure each customer has signed an acceptable MNDA.

Setting and Planning the Workback from Conception to Execution

In my experience, it takes a minimum of six months to plan and execute a world-class CAB. If you shorten the process, you'll likely not be able to achieve a world-class CAB. A company executive sponsor who's new to their role may ask for the in-person CAB meeting to happen within six to eight weeks, often because they're excited to learn from customers. If you're the CAB lead, I encourage you to push back and ask for a minimum of six months, especially if this is your very first CAB.

Why six months? CABs are time-consuming, and it's especially hard to develop content and ensure that people practice and prepare for the board meeting. Here are the main points that need to be completed within this time frame:

1. Form CAB goals

2. Create a CAB mission statement

3. Select internal executives

4. Select, pitch, and finalize customers

5. Set a budget and research and book approved venues, catering, transportation, entertainment, gifts, etc.

6. Select speakers and facilitators

7. Prepare executives, internal speakers, and facilitators, including reviewing presentation content and organizing rehearsal time

8. Create the CAB brand and content

9. Review CAB customer profiles together

10. Map out and finalize the day-of agenda, including icebreaker activities, one-on-one breakout sessions, and networking opportunities

It's possible to deliver a world-class CAB in less than six months, but don't underestimate the amount of time it will take to complete each of these tasks, and always plan for delays and hiccups.

1. Form CAB Goals

The company executive sponsor should tell the CAB lead about the C-suite's goals for the CAB. The CAB lead can also interview executives to determine what they want to learn from their customers.

Executives often have two main goals: The first is to get answers to questions that will help them validate an assumption. Here's a classic example. The company hosting the CAB sells security platforms. Their assumption is that functionality is just as important as the security features and that their customers will select a security platform that is easy for their employees to onboard and use. During the CAB, the company COO would like to ask the CAB customers if a greater investment in user design would generate more customers for their security platform and help the company become a market leader in the security industry.

The second goal is to get access to customers so they can hear firsthand what customers think of the company, observe how customers react to the presentation and questions to get to the root of issues, and hear how customers use products or services. Within the second goal, executives want a vetted group of customers to confide in and have deeper conversations with that provide answers they wouldn't receive from a customer satisfaction survey.

Here are two examples of executive goals:

a. A storage company that wanted to expand into the Asia-Pacific Japan (APJ) region had the following goals:

  ○ Create an Australian CAB composed of its early financial customers to gauge what features they like and how they're using the company's technology in their storage infrastructure.

  ○ Determine how to build out teams and best forecast sales in the APJ region.

b. A small start-up with only thirty paying customers at the time had the following goal:

  ○ Create a CAB of ten customers and hear firsthand how they use the company's product and to what other parts of their businesses the product could be applied.

2. Create a CAB Mission Statement

A CAB mission statement describes the purpose of the CAB meeting, and it is shared publicly with every participant. It sets the focus for each board member and expresses how much company executives value the customer board members. Without a mission statement, a CAB meeting may come across as a vendor sales meeting. A CAB mission statement also helps keep the meeting focused and on track. Here is one example of a mission statement:

To form a customer advisory board that validates executive technology strategies and fosters partnerships with our innovative customers.

Mission statements are crafted based on answers to the following two questions:

- Why have a CAB?

- What are the CAB goals?

Here are the responses that helped create the example mission statement:

Question	Example Response
Why have a CAB?	We're looking to grow our enterprise customer base in the next twelve months and file an initial public offering in the next two years.
What are the CAB goals?	We aren't sure how to develop our enterprise services and offerings. We want our customers to advise us on what services and offerings they want.

3. Select Internal Executives for the CAB Meeting

Ask your company executive sponsor to select which executives will be physically present at the CAB meeting. Many leaders may want a seat at the CAB table, but you might not have room for everyone. You should maintain a one-to-one ratio of company leaders to customers. This creates an intimate environment that helps customers feel open to giving constructive feedback. The company leaders who attend the CAB event will become executive sponsors for the customers.

The company leaders who typically attend a CAB are:

- chief executive officer

- chief operations officer

- chief revenue officer

- chief technology officer

- chief product officer

- chief customer officer or the head of support

- chief information officer

- chief product officer

- chief marketing officer

- vice president of product management (Optional)

- chief financial officer (Invite them, but they will likely not attend or will only ask to attend certain sessions.)

Once you've determined how much planning time you'll need, ask your company executive sponsor to pick a date for the CAB meeting outside of that window. Be sure to ask your executive sponsor if there are any factors or confidential events that could affect the CAB date. After they suggest a date, go to the chief of staff or the executive assistant (EA) to the CEO to review the suggested date. It's extremely useful to have an EA do this since they're constantly keeping track of events. If there's a conflict, the EA will be the best person to suggest an alternative date to ensure your C-suite will be able to attend.

Next, build out a high-level workback to go over with your company executive sponsor, including all the major milestones, such as review deadlines for the development of CAB content, dry run dates, and the final review of CAB content. (Use the example on page 44 to guide you. Additionally, you'll likely want to create a more granular workback of CAB-lead specific tasks for your own use.) Walk the company executive sponsor through an overview of the workback and what needs to get accomplished. By doing so, you can ask for their support if any issues arise. During this meeting, ask the company executive sponsor to help select which executives will be physically present at the CAB.

After you've met with the company executive sponsor, ask their EA to add CAB milestones to their calendar. The EA will be your partner throughout the CAB program. By partnering with the EA, you'll get time with the company executive sponsor to discuss content, address agenda changes, and get help with any issues. If your company has a chief of staff, invite them to sit in on the first meeting with your company executive sponsor. They will be a great resource, especially since they can act on your company executive sponsor's behalf.

Two days before the CAB meeting, have your company executive sponsor sign off on the final customer advisory board presentations.

The following sample workback shows one way to schedule the company executive sponsor's involvement.

Sample Workback: CAB Company Executive Sponsor's Involvement

CAB Stage	Timing & Due	Executive Sponsor Action	CAB Lead Action	Extra Details
Formalizing strategy: CEO sign-off on CAB strategy and customer board criteria	6 months before CAB meeting	CEO signs off on CAB Strategy and board criteria.	Create high-level pitch deck to nominate customers.	Ask the CEO who else should help with CAB nomination criteria.
CAB goals, mission statement, and agenda	5 1/2 months before CAB meeting	Sign off on goals, mission statement, and agenda.	Create internal and external CAB pitch deck to communicate CAB.	Agenda is high level for now, can be tweaked after finalizing who from the executive team is attending and presenting.
Review final CAB nominations, create finalist list, and settle on the number of customer board members	5 1/2 months before CAB meeting	Need to review CAB nominations list, settle on number of customers to have on board (6–10 customers).	Create a finalist CAB list. Reach out to finalists, CAB invite email (with a letter from the CEO, optional).	
Budget sign-off	5 months before CAB meeting	Review, ask questions, and sign off on budget.	Create budget.	

Finalize who on the executive team will attend the CAB	4 1/2 months before CAB meeting	Sign off on who is attending. Ask the CEO which customers they want to sponsor and with whom they want to have one-on-one meetings.	Create executive sponsorship responsibilities.	Consider: Does this change the agenda, the speakers? Do you need to invite an internal expert to co-speak with an executive?
Kickoff meeting for internal executives attending the CAB	4 months before CAB meeting	Review responsibilities, their roles (pre/ post), agenda, who is speaking.	Create a kickoff deck and ask the CEO to review it and help kick off this meeting to get everyone on the same page.	
Finalize speakers and agenda	3 1/2 months before CAB meeting	Sign off on final agenda and speakers; review final CAB customer list.	Start to program manage speakers.	
Dry run of CAB presentations	1 1/2 months before CAB meeting	Ask the CEO to attend, especially if C-suite does not have CAB experience.	Focus on who needs more help; find more resources if needed.	Last opportunity to make big changes to the agenda
Status update on CAB	1 month before CAB meeting	CAB lead provides an update of what is complete and what is a concern.	Suggest solution(s) to executive sponsor; request help.	

CAB Stage	Timing & Due	Executive Sponsor Action	CAB Lead Action	Extra Details
Review all customer profiles (all company CAB executives)	3 days before CAB meeting	All executives attending the CAB review all the customer profiles (in a spreadsheet format). Each executive is paired with a customer board member and will be considered that customer's executive sponsor post-CAB meeting.	Create CAB customer profiles that include what customers purchased, if there were any deals in the sales cycle, any recent support issues, their net promoter scores, and their background. Ask executives to be prepared to connect. Show them the boardroom layout and any meal assignments (they will get to sit near their CAB customer). Add that each executive team member needs to be ready to support the CAB during the event and afterward and should always be ready to answer question(s) from the board.	Invite all the executive assistants or record the meeting
Review and approve the final CAB presentation	2 days	You'll need a fresh set of eyes and an executive to review the final CAB presentation.	Work their executive assistant to block out time on their calendar.	This should be a must step. If the executive sponsor can't review, ask them to nominate another executive.
During CAB: group chat	Day of the CAB meeting	Ask the CEO to share their opinion(s).		

Post CAB	Day of the CAB meeting	The executive sponsor drives the meeting with all the internal company executives and assigns items for follow-up to each executive.	CAB lead writes out actions from the CEO meeting. Ask executives how they plan to follow up with CAB members.	Tracking post-CAB communication begins.
Review final CAB executive summary for customer and set next date for CAB meeting	48 hours after CAB meeting	Review CAB executive summary and have the CEO or EA write a thank you note to each customer board member. Confirm next date for a CAB or follow-up meeting to discuss any pending discussions from the CAB event.	Send out CAB executive summary to the customer board members. Follow CEO's directions for planning the next CAB.	

Select the Number of Days for the CAB Meeting

The number of days to allocate for a CAB meeting depends on your company's goals and budget.

In my experience, holding a CAB event over three days and two nights allows enough time for presentations, group sessions, breakout meetings, one-on-ones, and networking events. (Chapter 4 describes a three-day/two-night agenda in detail.)

If you lower your CAB expectations and focus on one or two goals, such as validate a company strategy and build rapport with customers, one can have a very successful one-day CAB. That said, it's important not to have long back-to-back meetings and risk losing everyone's focus and attention. Another option is to have a roadmap review of a new product to ask customers to become beta testers followed by breakout sessions, and a networking opportunity, such as lunch.

Executive Responsibilities

It's important to make sure everyone involved in the CAB understands their responsibilities. Executives can't expect to sit back and glide through the event. There's real work involved. After the CAB event, every company executive who attends will serve as a CAB sponsor. CAB executives have these responsibilities:

Pre-CAB:

- If they are presenting:
  - Take ownership of their presentation content and decide if they will speak or invite an expert to co-present. For example, the CEO may want to do the opening but will want the cofounder to present the company update.
  - Delegate who will work closely with them on their CAB presentation slides.
  - Attend presentation preparation meetings and rehearsals.
- Attend dry run CAB meetings.
- Review customer profiles and study their backgrounds.
- Speak with customers who request one-on-one calls with them.
- Accept the responsibility that they will have an ongoing relationship with customer advisory board members.

During the CAB:

- Be respectful of others' feedback, provide constructive criticism, and be curious.

- Listen and actively engage. Don't take calls or look at devices unless it's an emergency. Ask clarifying questions without a critical tone. Be grateful for the customer board members' presence.

- Take notes, especially follow-up notes for assigned customer board members.

Post-CAB:

- Attend the post-CAB internal meeting with other executives and the internal support team such as: product management, owners of features mentioned on the roadmap, product marketing, brand, designers, customer success, sales and customer support to gather feedback and actions. Be ready to follow up internally with more teams to share CAB customer findings.

- Reconnect with the CAB customer(s) assigned to them and follow up over video conference or by phone. Schedule quarterly check-ins. The executives will be called CAB sponsors after the first CAB meeting is over.

  o Record notes in the customer relationship management (CRM) system or pass the notes to the CAB lead or customer success manager to ensure the discussion between the executive and customer is logged.

- Support and respond to CAB customers when they reach out.

> **Executive Pro Tip:** Communicate company executive responsibilities to hold everyone accountable.
>
> Have your company executive sponsor present the CAB responsibilities to the executive team during a general management meeting, about four months before the CAB meeting, and add this to your workback. The executive sponsor should take about ten minutes and include a brief slide presentation. (The CAB lead can create the slides for the company executive sponsor.)

Select Customers for the CAB

When I was starting my marketing career at a network appliance start-up, my team was one other marketing person and me. I was fortunate enough to be a part of my company's first CAB. This board had ten customer board members, but one member was unable to attend the meeting because of a company emergency. What stood out was how everyone connected with one another during the event. It was special. Customers felt comfortable sharing, yet there were still enough customers to get different perspectives.

Determining the best number of customers and selecting the right customers is crucial to your CAB's success. Use the following guidance to help you select the best customers for your board.

Determine the Ideal Number of Customers

Figuring out how many customers to join your board is challenging.

If you're running a CAB for the first time, aim to have no more than ten customers for an in-person board. If you've been a part of a CAB in some shape or form and feel you can handle more customers, then perhaps add two more customers. These two must be known customers, which I define as customers with whom you have a good relationship and trust and who have had several one-to-one interactions with other company leaders. The two additional customers will help be advocates and speak up, especially when it's quiet in the room.

> **Executive and CAB Lead Pro Tip:** Don't just add more people for the sake of it.
>
> If you do, you may create an imbalance in the CAB.

Your executives or your head of sales may want to add more customers. Respectfully decline and share these reasons for keeping your CAB intimate:

- Executives can have authentic conversations with customers.

- In a small group, it's easier to get to the root of problems, and it's easier for executives and customers to collaborate.

- If the CAB is too big, it's very hard to form connections. If the customer board members don't feel comfortable, they won't share what they're thinking.

I've led a twenty-seven-person CAB, which I called a summit. The board members were a mix of new industry customers and retail, professional services, and global brand customers. Having this many people on the board created cliques, like in high school. The conversation was driven by only a handful of customers and executives. Sadly, the customers from whom we were seeking feedback became reserved. After the summit, I spoke to board members who had attended other CAB events. They shared with me that the summit board was too big, and the event was not intimate enough for people to speak candidly. I was not surprised at all. I apologized to the customers, thanked them for their honest feedback, and shared their comments with the executive team. Our executive team understood and decided to focus on having small business, midsize, and enterprise customer advisory boards.

Nominate Customers

From talking to your C-suite, you'll get a good sense of the type of customers they want on the board. Next, go to your sales and customer success leaders, who will be your best partners in building the board criteria.

Here are common criteria for a customer board member:

Criteria	Why?
A C-suite or VP customer who has innovative projects. (Direct level is fine if they carry themself as an executive.)	We want decision-makers on the board because they can explain their strategy down to the tactical steps of their projects.
An expert in their field who has extensive knowledge of business (such as having taken finance and accounting courses).	Customers who have a strong background in business are those who have higher success rates in meeting their goals.
Professionally articulate about product, industry, and company insights. (They're willing to speak up during discussions, not just listen.)	During a CAB, you want customers willing to open up and share and not be too shy. It bodes well for a higher experience for all board members if people speak up.
Constructive with feedback and respectful of colleagues.	At a CAB event, there will be people meeting for the first time and people from all backgrounds. It's best to have board members who are respectful and offer constructive feedback. You don't want abrasive or close-minded people setting the wrong tone and making people uncomfortable and unwilling to share. If there are disagreements, remind people to share their viewpoints without being reactive or making it personal. Encourage customers to come together with respect and empathy to share and learn. Healthy disagreements can heighten the value of the CAB.
Has previous experience sitting on a customer advisory board.	Customers with previous CAB experience are more comfortable speaking up and asking questions during the board meeting. They can also help moderate and/or facilitate a discussion.

CAB Lead Pro Tips: Working with sales and customer success leaders

1. **Don't skip the process of developing customer criteria.** Often, salespeople and customer success leaders become biased and have a few favorite customers. It's natural. However, your team owes it to the company to nominate all the best customers for the CAB.

2. **Avoid sales pitches.** Sales and customer success leaders will often want a sales presentation slide included in the CAB presentation. Be careful with these requests. Sales pitches can be a turnoff for customers. Coach sales and customer success that the focus of the CAB meeting is to build relationships between customers and executives.

Meet with Customer Nominees with a CAB Pitch Deck

If you're the CAB lead, you'll first need to develop a CAB pitch deck to break the ice with the nominated customer. This may seem like extra work, but it's never too early to start developing your CAB planning slides. You'll also need many of these pitch slides for internal communications to inform the team.

Here's what goes into the CAB pitch deck slides:

- The mission and purpose of the CAB

- The Agenda of your one-on-one meeting with the nominated customer

- Speak to any past CAB stories or cite this as your inaugural CAB.

- The CAB agenda

   o Mention that the agenda is about 80 percent complete and ask them for their thoughts on it. (You will have started working on the agenda as soon as the CEO signed off on the CAB customer criteria. Creating a strong agenda is so important to hosting a world-class CAB that I've dedicated the whole of chapter 4 to putting one together.)

- Any questions, concerns, or assumptions the customer wants addressed at the CAB meeting:

  o Take notes of all feedback. The feedback you get may help finalize your CAB agenda.

  o Provide and validate how well the customer knows your product and services.

- The customer's responsibilities for being on the board:

  o Ask them how they feel about the responsibilities. Use the questions in the next section to gauge each CAB nominee's temperament.

Ask Nominated Customers These Questions to Gauge Temperament

Asking your potential CAB advisers questions about their personality is super challenging—I get it. I only mastered this in my late thirties after going through a CAB with a global brand customer who glanced at his mobile phone all day and gave off the vibe that he was too good for our CAB. The fact that the company had flown him in from London (that is, spent a lot of money to have him attend the event) gave me the confidence to take charge of the customer-vetting process.

Interviewing each nominated customer is an essential practice. If you're the CAB lead, it's your job to make sure you have a high-functioning board. During calls with potential CAB customers, ask the following questions to confirm that the nominee is a good fit:

- What innovative projects would you share?

- Do you work closely with other business units and how? Who are the super users and super admins that use the technology that is spoken about at the CAB, and why?

- Do you feel comfortable speaking up in meetings? Can you articulate and openly share product, industry, and company insights?

If you're worried about asking these hard questions, practice with a colleague first. Lead by being genuine with the customer. Candidly share that it's up to the board executives and customers to openly communicate and collaborate to make the CAB meeting a success. It's not helpful for customers or executives to just be present. Also express the importance of respecting other board members' comments and providing constructive feedback.

Be Selective of Nominees: Jon the Account Rep Who Overstepped

While I was working on CAB nominations, a sales account representative, I'll call Jon, reached out to ask me about the CAB. I was excited that Jon was interested in the program. During the call, I learned that Jon had "promised" a CAB spot on the board to one of his customers because the customer asked for it. Alarm bells went off in my head.

I immediately told my manager, a senior vice president (SVP), that one of our ten prized spots on the board had been given away without our approval and then escalated it to our company executive sponsor. My manager reached out to the customer and asked him to participate in a marketing launch without mentioning the CAB. After the call, the manager updated me and Jon. I was surprised to learn that the manager was against having this customer join the CAB. He described the customer as brash and negative, and he didn't want that energy to be part of our next launch. The manager felt this nominee would be toxic for the board, and Jon had to go back to the customer and tell him that the board was full this year. The customer was upset, then asked Jon for discounts, which, of course, angered Jon.

I share this story because a CAB is a big investment, and it's crucial that the CAB lead talk to all nominated customers. Don't go by big brands or big titles that sales or executives may think will be great CAB members. In my experience some of the best CAB members came from small and midsize companies but were innovative and had vibrant personalities.

Communicate Customer Responsibilities

In tandem with the customer criteria, it's important to define the CAB customer responsibilities. Early on in my career, a peer from a big global company suggested I list all the activities the company executives wanted their CAB members to support. The company executives wanted the CAB customers to share their testimonials publicly, buy the company's complete solution, beta test, and the list went on and on. Clarifying customer responsibilities was a great tip, but since our company was not a global brand, I decided to focus them on practices that would help build relationships with company executives. These are the customer expectations I like to set and communicate in the CAB nominee pitch deck.

During the CAB:

- Be respectful of others' feedback, provide constructive criticism, and be curious. Listen and actively engage. Don't take calls or look at your devices unless it's an emergency.

- Advise on company direction, product, solutions, and services.

Post-CAB:

- Be available to talk to executives and company experts for the next six months to a year. (The time period would depend on your CAB program.)

- Be open to being approached for feedback within the next six months to a year and serve as a beta customer.

- Be willing to support future industry events and/or launches.

- Take reference calls to help win new customers.

There's a debate among CAB leads in the industry about listing the customer post-CAB responsibilities as a board member. My approach is to tailor these responsibilities to the customer's strengths and share example responsibilities with them. First, observe a customer board member, and then personally curate the highest value activities for that customer. Everyone's different. Some are introverted while others are extroverted. For example, have an introvert take a private call with an analyst or ask them to take a private reference call. For an extrovert who may like the limelight, find future speaking opportunities for them.

Address Customer Requests Before the CAB Meeting

Before the CAB, customers will often make a request to meet a company executive privately. Instead of waiting for the actual CAB to set up face-to-face meetings, offer to set up a pre-CAB video conference between the customer and an executive. Ask the customer directly what they want to talk about, so you can pull details or gather a backstory to make the time more fruitful. Also share with the customer that your leadership team is sincere about building a closer relationship with board members. These advance meetings can break the ice, dispel any nervous tension, and deepen rapport between customers and company executives.

Budgeting for the CAB Meeting

During times of economic hardship, it can be challenging to justify an in-person CAB meeting, but having an in-person event will set you apart from your competitors who are running virtual ones. I have worked with budgets of all sizes to create world-class in-person events. It may take an extra dose of creativity and effort to have a successful event on a modest budget, but it is doable. I'll share my CAB budget tips on page 62. First, let's review the top five CAB budget line items:

- Venue
- Food and beverage
- Travel
- Entertainment
- Gifts

Venues: Create an Experience

A primary reason I recommend six months to plan a CAB meeting is to allow adequate time to select a site and venue. You'll be competing with weddings and other business off-site meetings. The venue can make or break a customer's decision to spend one to two days with company executives, making it the main driver in the planning workback. Although almost everyone is burned out by virtual meetings and crave the in-person experience, you still need to choose a venue that makes it worth the customer's time and effort to attend.

Food and Beverages

As a CAB lead, I spent most of my budget on food, that's typically 35 to 40 percent of the budget. The quality of the food is always talked about, even more than the venue.

A key to meal planning is to think about what happens before and after the meal. For example, on the opening night, you may want to consider having a buffet and an open bar in a lovely garden or a room with a sweeping view to help facilitate networking among the board members. On the following morning, since people have had drinks, it's good to offer a hot breakfast to help soak up the liquor from the previous night.

Think about what snacks to have for breaks. There should be a mix of healthy and decadent treats. When people are networking, have the snacks in bite-size portions. Big cookies are fun to have, but when you eat one, you can't communicate. Provide coffee, tea, and mineral water. Mints are great to have at the snack station too.

Lunch should always be light because you don't want people to be sleepy in the afternoon. If people have flown in from different parts of the country, many may not have adjusted to the local time. If you pick a light lunch, make sure there are plenty of protein offerings in the afternoon break. You don't want hangry board members.

Dinner is different. Since there will likely be cocktails beforehand, wine served with dinner, and often drinks afterward, you'll want to have a heavier meal. The next morning, a hot breakfast with both sweet and savory offerings is best.

Most people will need to leave for the airport soon after the CAB meeting ends, so consider providing a gourmet lunch box, with a sandwich or quinoa bowl, a bag of chips, fresh-cut fruit, a cookie or a small tart, a little box of mints, another packaged snack for anytime on the journey, and wet wipes. These little details make the difference between a four-star and a five-star experience.

Travel Expenses

Travel budgets can easily add up to two thousand dollars or more per customer to mainly due to their lodging and flight to the CAB venue. Make sure you're factoring in ride-hailing services to and from the venue as well as other transportation and/or parking costs depending on the location. A good rule of thumb is to include sixty dollars per person in daily transportation costs.

Entertainment

Entertainment is nonnegotiable. These breaks from the business schedule keep people engaged and open up the opportunity for more fun ways to connect. A way to keep things simple is to ask the head chef of the restaurant or the sommelier to do a food demo or wine tasting of a particular region. Or go all out—once at a CAB in Napa, we had a sommelier take a very big champagne bottle and use a saber to open it and start the entertainment. The wine tour and dinner were in the $30,000 range. The range for entertainment is usually $150 to $700 per person. During the pandemic and the move to virtual CABs, companies hosted at-home wine tastings or hired baristas to teach people how to make the perfect cappuccino. For an in-person event, book meals or your venue in a location where you can add on a little experience. For example, hire a traveling massage therapist or provide a fun experience, like a live band. If you want to spend more than the recommended per-person range, I recommend shifting the dollars to gifting.

Gifts

Many people who put on a CAB like to give high-end sports jackets, like a fancy fleece and windbreaker shell, but it's too common. Instead, I opt for a few select, curated gifts for each customer board member. The budget range for gifts is usually $50 to $150 per person.

Depending on your budget, you can have an in-room snack and handwritten card or provide a gift bag at check-in. Include small snacks, water (if the hotel will allow it), and a company logo gift. The logo gift will depend on the time of year and where you're having the meeting. For example, if your event is in New York City, you'll want to provide a map of the closest attractions, a beanie if it's cold, and a water bottle.

Give with thoughtfulness. Make it personal. Don't be afraid to ask your customers about their hobbies. Here are a couple of alternative gift scenarios:

- **Make it a team sport:** I had a customer who ran a large nonprofit team. He asked me not to give him gifts. He suggested a couple of $50 gift cards that he could raffle or give to his team as a thank-you. That was easy for me to offer, and I will always remember how genuinely excited he was to give them to his team.

- **Find out about their charitable affiliations:** A hoodie or the newest tech gadget didn't feel right for a particular customer who coached a soccer team. Instead, we donated a $150 gift card for Dick's Sporting Goods so he could buy soccer equipment for his players.

- **Is one of your customers a dog or cat person?:** One customer loved their black lab, Momo. We looked on Etsy and found someone who could paint a custom portrait of his prized pup. I asked to see a photo of Momo and sent it to the painter. They then mailed the painting directly to the customer. We spent sixty dollars, and the customer was so touched by the portrait that he hung it in his hallway with all his family photos.

It's great to give, but it's not about how much. It's how much thought you put into each gift. Please don't give another hoodie unless, of course, the customer specifically asks for one. Surprise the customer. They will always be grateful and touched by a personalized gift.

CAB Budget Tips

Here are some tips to help you have a world-class CAB on a modest budget:

- If flying customers to the venue is too expensive, consider having two smaller CAB meetings and splitting up the executives. These days, executives live all over the world. Fly them to your company headquarters and invite customers in a twenty-mile radius to attend. To save even more, host them for just half a day. That way, you'll sponsor only one meal. Snacks and drinks will cost a lot less too. Alternatively, select a big city with the highest concentration of customers that fit your criteria. For example, Chicago has a lot of headquartered offices downtown. You can easily have a CAB at a coworking space if your regional office is too small.

- Midweek is a good option for hotels, and there's often the possibility of negotiating a discount.

- The cost of a rented mansion on a vacation rental site, like Airbnb, can be half the cost of a traditional hotel.

- Save on entertainment by combining it with a meal at a restaurant. Call the restaurant and ask if they will work on creating an experience. Maybe the chef will let everyone make ravioli together, or you could ask the chef to do a demo. Or if they have a bar, it could be a bar trick, a wine tasting, or a mixology class. You can save thousands of dollars on entertainment, and it will be way more fun and intimate to have it at a restaurant.

- In some cases, the cost of booking a coworking space for an event is almost the same as booking a restaurant. With coworking spaces, you'd need to organize lunch offsite, so do your research and keep in mind a restaurant could be the more economical option.

- The biggest way to save is to have the meeting at a headquarters or a regional office that your business already leases. This is ideal if you're only hosting a one-day event, no hotel needed.

- Trim from the gift budget. Remember, it's the thought that counts, not the sticker price.

Being world-class doesn't necessarily equate to spending lots of money. It does mean providing a thoughtful and personalized experience. Focus on what each customer values. For example, I had a customer who was into gardening, so as a gift I bought them heirloom seeds to take home to sow. Another customer was a coach for a disadvantaged youth soccer team, and I offered to sponsor their jerseys. Personalization wins. And it's not just meaningful when it comes to gift-giving, but in the way you prioritize relationship building. Focus on getting to know the customer as a person and not just as a professional contact throughout the CAB meeting.

Selecting a Venue and Layout for your CAB

Think outside of the box when selecting a venue. A big hotel is the default option for a CAB meeting, but it's not always the best choice. Prioritize a unique experience and smaller, more intimate venues. You can also save big by avoiding hotels. Hotels make big money on banquets, and there's usually a minimum spend to secure a room block or conference space. Consider more personal venues.

A restaurant with a view in a great location

Picture Half Moon Bay, California, a seaside resort town, as the location of choice. You could opt to have all the events at the five-star Ritz-Carlton. Or you could consider having dinner at a family-run Italian restaurant that's within walking distance of the beach.

A vacation rental versus a resort

For a smaller CAB meeting, why not explore renting designer homes or beautiful properties in scenic places? You can host your CAB on the property and hire local caterers. Make sure everyone has a private room. Sharing is a big no. The vacation rental route removes the need to meet food and beverage contract minimums. You can also say goodbye to resort fees and late checkout woes.

Rent off-site space

Maybe you have a regional office that's close to a coworking space. Let's take Chicago, for example, where there are several coworking locations. If you are the CAB lead, look for airy and large rooms where the furniture is on wheels to make moving it easy. A location that is close to a restaurant or an experience is a plus.

In-Person CAB Meeting Layout

In my experience, a U-shaped seating layout is ideal for a twenty-person CAB meeting (my recommended number based on ten executives and ten customers), and you should keep this layout in mind as you research venues. Speakers will present at the open end of the U, and you'll want to make sure the U is spacious enough to provide roomy seating for everyone. There will also need to be room for three seats at the back for the CAB lead and two notetakers.

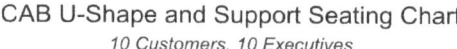

CAB U-Shape and Support Seating Chart
10 Customers, 10 Executives

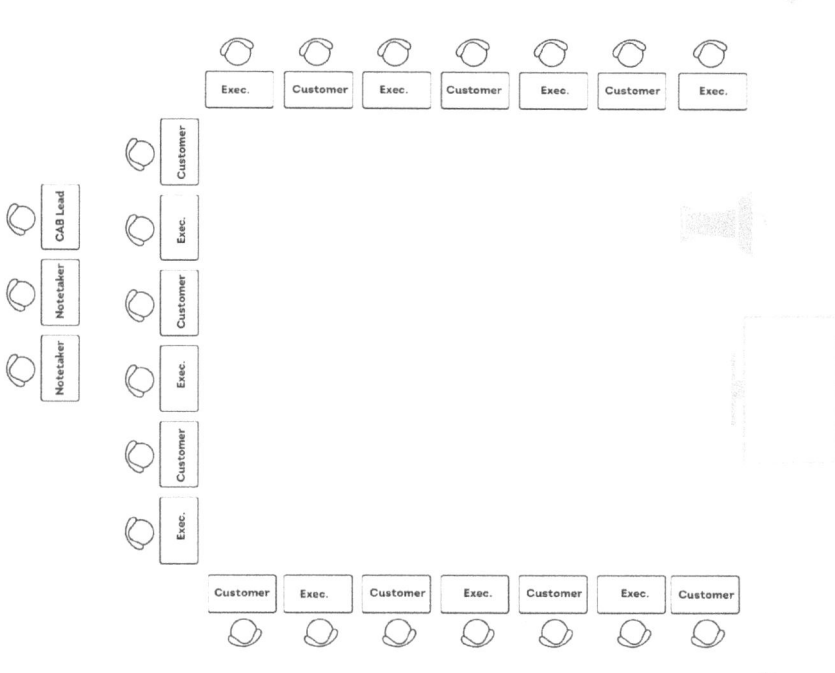

When you're researching venues online and speaking to the salesperson of the venue, make sure you share the U-shape seating idea. Often, smaller venues won't have tables or chairs to fit the room comfortably, and you may need to use narrow rectangular tables to build the U shape. Holding the CAB meeting in a fixed boardroom table at the host company's office is one way to help lower the cost, however, most of these rooms comfortably fit only eight to twelve people around an oval table. Imagine your ten customers at a board table and ten of your executives sitting around the table feeling cramped—or having to ask executives to sit in the back of the room. It's not ideal.

Depending on the size of the meeting, it may be best to have two large rooms, one for the U-shaped general sessions and the other for brainstorming or activity breakouts.

Pros and Cons of Venues

Each venue has its pros and cons. Let's look at each venue:

Hotel pros:

- Easy bid system, and they often have event managers on-site to answer questions.

- Hotel staff to help you plan your CAB experiences along with services for food and beverage, audio and visual (AV), and concierge.

- Hotels, especially boutique or luxury hotels, are in premium locations, such as the Mandarin Oriental in the Back Bay of Boston or the iconic Plaza Hotel in New York, at the corner of Central Park and Fifth Avenue.

Hotel cons:

- It's expensive overall for the venue. There are minimums to meet for food and beverage.

- Lower quality of food, high cost for seafood.

- The legal contract can be tricky. Have your legal team or lawyer review it.

- Stricter cancellation dates and penalties.

Coworking space pros:

- Can scale down in space. Services are often easy to order.

- Buildings are clean and modern. No need to worry about AV systems.
- Located in major cities.

Coworking space cons:

- Premium space costs can be high, not including local tax.
- Costs can increase quickly (coffee and snacks).
- Service isn't always consistent.
- Often no opportunity to negotiate on price, especially if there's a demand.

Vacation rental pros:

- Secluded, special, more relaxed atmosphere.
- Can save up to 30 to 50 percent of the price of a hotel.

Vacation rental cons:

- Lots of logistics to manage (parking, private chef, house assistant or manager) that could add more costs.
- Often everything can be booked in an app (such as with Airbnb and Vrbo).
- The vacation rental manager service will vary. There's a risk that the manager may not service your needs before the actual CAB meeting.
- May need to hire additional support such as a chef, drivers, and delivery people.
- Mansions often have a three-night minimum.

Restaurant pros:

- Lots of restaurants to choose from. Negotiations are a possibility, such as the room rental being waived if you spend more at the restaurant.

- Flexibility of banquet style.
- Have a creative experience, such as having the chef do a demo.
- Post-CAB possibility: Have the kitchen put together dinner for each family as a thank-you (instead of buying a gift).

Restaurant cons:

- The restaurant may not have enough space or be willing to let you bring in your own AV equipment.
- Your chosen restaurant may not have a private room.
- Parking may be difficult. May have to pay for valet or your own parking lot.

Regional or HQ pros:

- Most cost-effective venue. (Your company already pays for the rent.)
- Customers get to see firsthand what the company and its culture is like.
- Opportunity to bring in special staff to meet with customers. (A special customer could finally meet their CSM in person or a support engineer who was extremely helpful, fostering more connection.)

Regional or HQ cons:

- It may be difficult to inform building facilities people, office managers, reception, and others that there are customer VIPs in the building.
- Catering is required, and you may need party equipment. There's lots to juggle, and office staff may not want to help. Ask your company executive sponsor to help interoffice teams to support the CAB.

Selecting Speakers and Facilitators

It's important that all CAB meeting speakers have a presence and be able to engage the board members when they speak. Speakers who are dull will quickly lose the board's interest. Don't settle for mediocre speakers. CABs are a significant investment of money and time. The customer board members deserve thoughtful, compelling, and engaging content and experiences. First let's focus on the internal CAB speakers.

The first speaker should be the CEO, a cofounder, or the general manager to set the tone. They should welcome the board to ask questions during the presentation and encourage constructive feedback.

Select facilitators who are good at reading the room. Choose leaders who are comfortable allowing and encouraging others to talk, and who know how to keep the discussion going. Take the time to find someone on your internal team to be a facilitator. Alternatively, you could invite a veteran CAB customer to facilitate, but note, just because they're great at providing feedback doesn't mean they're good at facilitation. Ask them candidly how much experience they have in facilitating.

Dennis, the chief revenue officer we met in chapter 1, had this to share about the importance of selecting dynamic and engaging speakers:

At a start-up, I didn't ask to review the agenda and the speaker lineup. To my surprise, we had one of our very intellectual VPs present a section of the roadmap. Within five minutes of them presenting, I looked around the room and the board's eyes were glazed over. I never want that experience for our customers again. Speak up, and advocate for your customers.

Preparing Executives, Internal Speakers, and Facilitators for the CAB Meeting

Let's address the elephant in the room. Your executives want a CAB, *but* it will be a challenge to get them to do the "work" to develop their presentations, review the customer board profiles, and prepare to be active participants at the board meeting. Wrangling the leadership team is even more of a challenge because the CAB lead is usually someone who's junior to the executives. This is why it's important for the company executive sponsor to set expectations with other executives early on, about four months before the CAB meeting.

Internal Presentation Support and Best Practices

One way to make sure all company executives who will be presenting at the CAB meeting are prepared is to make sure they have all the resources they need to write their presentation and create the accompanying slides. Most executives, including the CEO who will provide the opening remarks, may already have presentations that can easily be adapted for the purposes of the CAB meeting, but others, such as the executive sponsor of the CAB who will usually give a company overview presentation, may need to start from scratch. In that case, pair the executive with the relevant resource— such as a chief of staff, vice president, manager, or graphic designer— to work on their presentation. It's crucial to check in on each speaker to make sure they hit each milestone deadline and are on track to complete their presentation on time.

Here are some best practices to consider when creating CAB-facing presentations and slides for your esteemed customers:

- Remind executives to tailor their presentations and slides to the CAB customers and not simply repurpose slides they have been using for sales presentations or other purposes.

- Don't make the CAB company presentation one hundred-plus slides. Executives often provide too many details in slides and don't leave enough time for discussion, which is the purpose of the CAB meeting.

- Create one or two slides with details to provide an overview, but spend time facilitating questions to help validate assumptions with your customer advisory board.

- Create slides that have an assumption, for example: "Customer surveys have told us our billing is hard to understand," with a pie chart of the feedback. Then have the executive explain their thoughts on the pie chart and prompt the customers to provide their opinion.

- Curate the slides to have breaks and engagement. The presentation should be high-level and encourage discussion.

- Coach the executive(s) to pause after they present a slide to observe and ask the board what they think.

- Build slides with the intention of hearing customers' thoughts, whether that's the current competition, market, or strategy.

- Anticipate tough questions and be prepared to answer them.

Remember, the CAB meeting isn't meant to be a big "show-and-tell." It's meant to connect the board and executives, form bonds and trust, and open dialogue about confidential information. Creating presentations and slides with these best practices in mind will not only help you develop relationships with your customers but also create partnerships and encourage customers to seek advice from your company.

Customer Guest Speaker— Picking the Right Customer

Selecting the right customer to speak at a CAB meeting is extremely challenging. Your executive team will want a big-brand customer to speak to how innovative they are by using the company's products, services, and/or solution. I typically focus on how the customer tells the story, whether the story is compelling, and whether it fits the CAB themes. For example, I knew of a customer who was using one of our products in the field and had great success with it. It changed the way they worked and communicated and helped make them more profitable. This customer was a VP of IT. He was intense, dynamic, fit, and confident. However, he didn't come from a well-known company. I fought for this customer to be our customer keynote. I wanted to showcase a customer who had found exceptional business value from one of our undervalued products.

External Presentation Support and Best Practices

External presentation support and best practices are almost the same as internal presentation support and best practices, but with a big dose of marketing support. If you have a customer guest speaker (usually as a keynote speaker), I always offer to create their presentation. Here are the steps.

1. Interview them, get down their entire story, and get it transcribed. Ask them for their company's brand guidelines.

2. Go back, listen to the interview, and read the transcription. Print out the transcription and start making notes for a draft of the presentation deck.

3. Create a mock-up of the customer's presentation. In the presentation notes, consider pasting direct quotes from

your interview to help the customer recall exactly what they shared.

4. Ask the company's designer to create a "keynote" presentation for the customer (keeping the quotes from the interview in the notes section).

5. Have a meeting with the customer to review the presentation. I also like to invite an executive who will attend the CAB. The executive will act as a new set of eyes to review the presentation and a cheerleader to thank and pump up the customer. They can also give constructive feedback.

6. Have a final dry run of the presentation with the customer and the executive. The customer may have questions about the CAB, so if you haven't done so, show them the final agenda and remind them of the importance of their customer keynote. If possible, share an example. For instance, at a previous CAB meeting, I had invited a customer to give the keynote on his experiences using our company's mobile feature. Our executives had more mobile strategies that they wanted to validate with our customer board members. Opening the CAB meeting with a customer mobile story helped our other customers open up about their use cases. The customer's keynote mobile story also provided a concrete example of how they changed the way they worked in the field and how they profited from using our mobile features.

Who Approves the Content?

The company executive sponsor of the CAB has the final approval. As the senior leader, they oversee the CAB. It's their role to review and provide feedback on slides.

Since all executives get pulled eight different ways every day, the CAB lead should give ample warning for when final slides must be done and carve out enough time in the schedule for the executive sponsor to review everything.

Open up a chat stream with all the presenters and those who created presentations, including the graphic designers, so the executive sponsor can tag and ask for clarification or suggest changes. Timely communication is very important because all presentations must be finalized before the CAB meeting starts.

Ask Your Leaders to Rehearse

It may be difficult to ask executives to rehearse in front of the internal CAB team, but it's essential. CAB meetings are typically held once a year, so executives don't get a lot of practice. Many will try to wing it, which is never a good idea. The stakes are too high. It's very important to practice in front of the group. It will help executives master the CAB meeting content, and they will find it easier to engage with and ask sincere questions of the customer board members.

If you're finding it challenging to pin down executive speakers to rehearse, or just have a sense that they won't show up to the dry run, ask your company executive sponsor to step in. For example, ask the company executive sponsor to have a one-on-one with the executive to review the presentation.

Creating the CAB Meeting Brand and Content

Each CAB meeting should have a unique brand identity: colors, slide design, and a logo. The CAB meeting needs to be elevated to an executive VIP event. Customers need to know and feel they were handpicked to provide constructive feedback to the executives. The CAB brand also reminds executives and the teams who build the CAB meeting content that this is a high-profile experience. Encourage the CAB logo to be added to the CAB customers' LinkedIn profiles.

In my experience, the company overview and product/demo sessions will need the most slide design support. To give all teams enough time to create content, make sure to set up a meeting with the head of creative to ask for resources up front and provide them with all relevant CAB meeting deadlines.

Branding a CAB meeting presentation and its logo helps to set the tone of the board and should continue on location. For a customer advisory board hosted along the shores of Monterey, California, my team used ocean blue for our brand color and named our breakout rooms with logos of local sea life: Octopus, Sea Otter, and Shark.

All slides should match the slide design style. This means making sure all executive presenters submit their final slides on time so the design team has enough time to do their work. If you're asking a customer to present during the CAB, offer for your designer to help with the layout of the presentation and align the content with the CAB meeting's style. Elevating your customer slides will give a positive boost to your customers' egos and they will be excited to present at the CAB.

Reviewing the CAB Customer Profiles with the Executive Team

About three days before the CAB event, arrange a meeting for every executive who will be attending the CAB event to review each customer board member's account background.

Here's an example of how you can pull a report from a CRM that shows the account, product details, and any current issues such as support ticket statuses. I call this report the CAB Customer Dashboard/Profiles. After the CAB meeting, you'll use this to help your executives follow up and track their communications with their assigned CAB customer as well as share how their relationship is faring.

CAB Customer Dashboard/Profiles

Name	Ron Peni
Title	CIO
Email	rp@xp.com
Company/ Industry	XP/ Consulting
Product in use	1, 2, 3, 4
Professional Services	Yes, for custom onboarding
Current Sales Opportunities	Stage 4: three more products of 1
Support tickets?	Yes, tier 1 (days open 2)
Rep/CSM/ PS	Kim P./ Mike M./ Gary S.
Global?	Brazil and Japan
Partner	IBM

Additional Best Practices for Planning a World-Class In-Person CAB

Amazing venues are memorable, but what I learned from putting on nine different company CAB programs is that it's the details that will make your CAB event stand out. Put in the time to get to know your customers and be extra thoughtful by anticipating their needs. Don't skip these steps.

These are a few additional best practices to help you create your world-class CAB.

Accommodate Your Customers

Be attentive to what people enjoy. For example, one CAB meeting coincided with the National Hockey League Stanley Cup playoffs. I learned that one of our CAB members played hockey in college, so I brought in a TV during our networking happy hour event. All the hockey fans from the board were overjoyed and were able to connect over their shared passion of hockey before the CAB meeting had even started.

At another CAB event, many members were jet-lagged from their international flights, so we found a café that served espressos to help them stay awake through the end of the day.

Be Flexible

Even if you have a minute-by-minute itinerary, make the necessary adjustments to take care of your customers and help them enjoy their experience.

Make it easy for those who have dietary restrictions by asking if anyone has any food allergies or what their drink preferences are ahead of the CAB meeting. Make sure CAB members who don't drink alcohol are given a highball glass with soda water and a slice of lime. People are so grateful for these personal gestures. It shows that you thought of them and made them feel just as important as those whose glasses are filled with champagne. And the customer doesn't have to explain why they aren't drinking.

Have Good Air Circulation

Have you ever sat through a sixty-minute meeting in a room so airless that you couldn't concentrate? A room with great air circulation is a must. Providing a comfortable setting means people will pay attention to what's happening in the room, not to the room itself.

Provide Networking Opportunities

Over the years, customers have told me what they valued most from a CAB meeting was the networking opportunities. Ask company executives to facilitate conversations and help customers get to know each other by introducing them. This is a great way to bring shy customers together.

Additionally, company leaders need to set a fun, friendly, and encouraging atmosphere for the customers to feel welcome to share. Make sure you have a pre-CAB meeting for all the internal company CAB attendees and spend a good part of the meeting reviewing their roles during the breakouts or sessions. Remind them to pause, listen actively, and speak less. Having company leaders who are prepared and mindful will set your CAB event apart.

Plan the Seating Chart to Support Requests

It's very common for the C-suite and customers to request to talk to executives and vice versa. An easy way to plan your seating chart is to put two customers on either side of a company executive. For your VIP customer who's willing to be a guest speaker, ask them which executive they would like to meet and chat with and then seat them next to each other. That way, it's easier for them to make a connection and have a deeper conversation. Before the CAB meeting, make sure you brief the executive and prepare them to meet the customer. If there are multiple customer board members who want access to an executive, give priority to the guest speaker by offering a private breakfast with the executive or a one-on-one meeting.

If you want to foster peer-to-peer connections among customers, encourage customers to sit in front and ask executives to sit in the back. Have a seat right in the front for the next speaker, who could be a customer or company executive. Many executives may object to sitting in the back. You'll have to consult with your company executive sponsor to know how the other executives will receive the idea.

Breaks can be tricky. If you have breaks, often people will spend more time chatting and not head back to their seats. It's a good thing for networking, but bad for the pace of the CAB meeting. Arrange for a chime to sound, to remind people to go back into the board meeting.

Mix up the seating at mealtimes to help everyone network. CABs have a high social component, and people tend to connect on a deeper level when they share common ground. For example, I sat two people next to each other who were from different industries, but both grew up in Texas.

Choose World-Class Venues

Amazing venues are memorable, but the details are what really stand out. No matter where you decide to hold the CAB meeting, consider the experience from the point of view of each board member and do what you can to elevate it. While the CAB lead does the bulk of the planning, ask the head of events or field marketing for support, especially since they're much more savvy with event negotiations.

Chapter 3 covered the following:

- The internal roles you need to plan a successful in-person CAB.

- The process and best practices of planning your CAB and selecting executives and customers.

- How to communicate responsibilities to your executives and customers.

- Creative ways you can budget for the venue, food and beverage, travel, entertainment, and gifts.

In the next chapter, you'll learn the most important components of planning a CAB: the agenda, including the elements of a CAB agenda and how to create your own.

4

THE WORLD-CLASS IN-PERSON CAB EVENT AGENDA THAT CREATES TRUST AND HUMAN CONNECTION

Your in-person two-day/three-night CAB event agenda will likely include several standard elements, such as an opening, presentations, discussions, breaks, and a closing. But how you schedule and execute these elements and additional networking components will make your CAB world class. In this chapter, you'll learn how to develop a CAB agenda so your company can quickly build trust with its customers and meet its goals.

Here's an example of a world-class CAB event agenda:

*** **Day 1** ***

Afternoon Arrival

Evening Kickoff Cocktails (drinks and small bites, to encourage networking)

Welcome/Icebreaker Activity

*** **Day 2** ***

Morning: Opening of the CAB Meeting and Welcome

Company Overview (In-Depth)

CAB Discussion Point 1

Midmorning: Break

CAB Discussion Point 2

Lunch

Customer Guest Speaker

Product or Service Roadmap Part 1

Midafternoon: Break

Product or Service Roadmap Part 2

Business Operational Review

Closing with Acknowledgment

Evening Event (Dinner, Experience)

*** **Day 3** ***

Breakfast Meetings (one-on-one meetings between customers and executives)

Customer Presentations, new updates from other business units

CAB Event Closing

Internal Executive Follow-Up Meeting

CAB adjourned to make afternoon flights

Now, let's break down some world-class ways to approach each of these elements.

Afternoon Arrival

When the CAB members arrive, have a table set up to give them a gift bag, answer any questions they may have, and review the evening and the agenda with each customer. Some customers may just want to go to straight to their room. Read how the customer is feeling. You can skip the review of the agenda, but tell them where to meet up for the Evening Kickoff event.

Evening Kickoff Cocktails (Drinks and Small Bites to Encourage Networking)

Planning a cocktail party with plenty of food makes for easy networking opportunities for each board member. Remember that not everyone drinks alcohol. Include mocktails on the cocktail menu. If you have vegetarians, make sure they have plenty to eat, and don't put their food right next to a meat-carving station. These are little but important details to make your board feel special.

Welcome/Icebreaker Activity

When the board has all arrived at the cocktail event, the CAB lead will signal to the company executive sponsor to ask people to gather around. In my experience, it's better to ask people to stand in a circle or semicircle, so everyone on the board can make eye contact. The company executive sponsor will introduce themselves and welcome everyone, and then ask everyone to participate in an icebreaker. The icebreaker is meant to get everyone to open up. It's not meant to be torture, so pick a light and fun activity. For example, use one of these questions to get the conversation going:

- What is your favorite band or play?
- If you could pick up a new skill in an instant, what would it be and why?

Morning: Opening of the CAB Meeting and Welcome

The evening event is to help customers get to know executives and other customers as people, to learn a little about themselves and not just about their roles at work. When day two begins, customers and executives will be more comfortable and more willing to listen intently since they have gotten to know the other board members.

Before the opening remarks, offer a breakfast for more networking. Some customers like to pull executives aside there because they feel more comfortable asking them questions. It's often hard for the board to get settled because they are enjoying networking.

This is why it's crucial to have an opening and welcome on the morning of Day 2: it helps to set the tone of the CAB meeting and to get customers to focus on the agenda. The opening generally includes a welcome remark, which could be a story of the founding of the CAB, a review of the agenda, and any announcements.

It's critical that the CAB starts off with the correct tone so customers feel respected and open to speaking up. Whoever says the opening must give a sincere, warm welcome and be excited about the CAB. Since customers expect to connect with leaders of your company, it's best to ask a founder or C-suite executive, such as your CEO or COO, to do the opening and welcome.

During a CAB I led, an executive who was set to open the CAB was upset for some unknown reason. He was wearing his emotions on his face, which would have been a negative way to open the CAB.

I made the decision to ask the founder to step in to do the welcome and review of the agenda. If I didn't make that change, customers may have felt apprehensive to share during the CAB.

Company Overview

A company overview should help build board members' trust in the company executives and set the tone for the day. Only when there is trust will customers' listen, learn, and advise. The company executive sponsor typically presents and needs to be authentic and vulnerable to build a safe environment where everyone feels comfortable sharing feedback and ideas.

In the first part of the overview, the company executive sponsor shares the key decisions and turning points that have shaped the company's current strategy and openly shares what the company is planning for the future. This information is for board members only and should be kept confidential.

In the second part of the overview, the sponsor should explain why the company needs advisers at this point in time and describe their concerns.

Have your company executive sponsor deliver the company overview with humility and sincerity. One of the most effective overviews I ever heard was given by a founder who began by talking about the founding of the start-up and then shared how he planned to grow the company. He openly shared that he and the management team felt competition was at their heels. The management team wanted to have this CAB to really understand how customers felt. He spoke to the board as if he were speaking to his friends. He asked if the board could validate areas where the company should put more investment and advise on which priorities to act on to keep their competitive advantage.

By being up front and honest, your executives will develop deeper connections with the CAB customers. Later, your customers will be more willing to reciprocate as customer advocates.

CAB Discussion Point 1

After the company overview, block off time for a discussion session. Often companies like to go straight into presentations on the product or service, but I would encourage the CAB lead to provide an opportunity for executives and customers to discuss a topic of company concern. For example, if executives want to hear what the customers think of the company, pick an issue from your customer satisfaction survey, such as how long it takes to resolve support tickets.

A known issue is a good place to start because it provides a natural opening for executives to listen to customer feedback. Executives may also ask customers more questions to help them resolve the issue.. Having a collaborative discussion builds another layer of trust, and this may lead to customers wanting more one-on-one time with executives.

Time for a Break: Midmorning and Afternoon

Breaks help relieve the intensity of discussions and provide a networking opportunity. Use breaks to form connections between company leaders and customers. It's their time to network with each other. Executives may be able to ask a customer what they thought. Or customers may now feel like they can confide in a company leader.

I suggest having one break midmorning and another in the afternoon. Make sure you plan them so there aren't too many back-to-back talks.

One minor, but important, detail is how much time to allocate for a break. Don't give too long or too short a break. Ten to fifteen minutes is ideal. Make sure you give people time to use bathroom facilities and get a drink and/or snack. If the bathroom is far, put the drinks and snacks inside the meeting room to help keep the day on schedule.

CAB Discussion Point 2

This discussion point can be a "testing the waters" or a "new strategy" discussion. Refrain from calling it a brainstorm, although it's often a term that's brought up. A CAB adviser once reminded me that most customers aren't great at brainstorming, especially in groups. Brainstorming may also be uncomfortable for most board members. Only a handful of customers may take the lead while everyone else sits back and watches. With CAB time limited, it's better to develop questions to facilitate feedback and advice from the board.

If you're having a hard time deciding on your second discussion point, you can focus on discussing company growth and/or direction.

Or you can adjust the format of this discussion point session by having a customer board member co-facilitate with a company leader. Here's how this played out in a CAB I organized: The company hosting the CAB was focused on transitioning from selling to midsize companies to enterprise companies. The customer board member was one of the company's first enterprise customers and he candidly shared his experience helping the company understand what levels of services and needs to anticipate in order to serve enterprise customers, which ultimately led to hosting a CAB with enterprise customers. The brief storytelling by each speaker (without slides) communicated to the rest of the board that this company was genuinely interested in learning from them.

Alternatively, you can invite an expert in your company who isn't an executive to co-lead with an executive or customer. They can talk about their beta experience. We once had an IT director from a UK government agency and our SVP of Services talk about how they had to make changes to their beta program to support government agencies, and that led to early adoption of the technology.

No matter which format you choose, remember that these CAB discussions are meant to create a safe, inclusive space so board members feel welcome and respected for their advice.

A great time to break for lunch is right after the second discussion point. Lunch serves as an opportunity for more networking. I often set the seating chart and have executives sit next to customers they want to get to know or customers they have been assigned to sponsor. Customers are also interested in strategically meeting other board members, so I also try to accommodate customers who have asked to sit next to a specific executive (and if that's not possible, arrange a private meeting for them). Lunch is a great time for executives to learn more about a customer's business and for customers to build a relationship with executives to support their business based on all the confidential information shared with them.

The Importance of the Second Half of the CAB (Afternoon)

By this time, you've built trust with your board and they feel settled and comfortable sharing and speaking up. Now's the right time to ask the hard questions or validate strategies. The second half of the day is when more board members open up and ideas are shared and formed.

Executives and product, service, and customer leaders don't typically get access to customers in a board format, so they are often eager for the afternoon sessions. Customers generally don't get this time with executives or product leaders for feedback either (unless there's a major problem), and they usually have questions they want answered. Customers tend to look forward to the afternoon as much as the company leaders.

The next three to four hours is when both customers and executives will truly learn, validate, and explore ideas as a board. Value the second half of the CAB; it can be a time to get to the root of issues, confide in the customers, and receive constructive feedback. Use the afternoon to ask the board what they think in real time and drill deeper by asking more questions on the spot to get input.

Keep in mind that the customers are listening to and observing your company executives. They will be mentally evaluating your company as a vendor. Customers want to leave feeling confident of the investment they've made with your company. And they also want confirmation that they should continue renewing and/or increasing their spend with the company. Often it takes a combination of the CAB product or service roadmap presentation, one-on-one conversations with executives, and peer feedback during the CAB event for the customer to decide whether to continue investing—or not.

The afternoon session includes four components to build on the foundation of trust and connection established during the morning meetings: a customer guest speaker, the roadmap, business review breakout meetings, and a closing with acknowledgment.

Customer Guest Speaker

It's often a big challenge to be the "hall monitor" and get everyone back to their seats after lunch. I've found that one way to smooth this transition is to have a customer (a board member) speak immediately following lunch. There's something about having a peer speak that will make all the board members quietly and respectfully take their seats.

Inviting a customer to speak is also a great way to set the tone of the second half of the CAB event. The first half of the day was focused on providing updates and asking questions pertinent to the vendor's business. A presentation by a customer guest speaker shifts the focus to the customer's story and needs.

The customer guest speaker should be someone who can share an experience completing a new project or a successful strategy that segues naturally into the next session. If you don't have a customer who is a good fit to speak on the themes of the CAB meeting, invite a customer or other company executive with an impressive career who's an engaging speaker to start the afternoon on a positive and upbeat note.

I've also asked guest speakers to help end the CAB. Even a mature, well-planned CAB program can run into issues. This happened to me during an afternoon board meeting. The head of product had to deliver news of the new product being delayed. I didn't want to have a big negative cloud hanging over our evening event. Instead, I diffused some of the negativity by adding a positive speaker. I found a chief technology officer (CTO) customer in the construction business willing to talk about their company's innovations and how they use the vendor company's product differently in the field. While the board was not happy with the delays, they understood, and the closing customer keynote created excitement about how to support employees in the field. While what I did can be perceived as total deflection, my goal for the CAB is to create experiences. I wanted the evening to be more open and balanced.

Executive Pro Tip: Engage with customers who are reserved and shy and make them feel special.

Observe your board members during happy hour or dinner. Talk to customers who seem reserved, have a pensive grin, or display folded arms, and ask them if they want to speak directly with an executive. You can't make everyone happy, but you can reach out and sincerely try to make your board members feel welcome and valued.

Product or Service Roadmap

The product or service roadmap is the company blueprint of up-and-coming new enhancements or new products or services that the company is planning to build. Customers look forward to the roadmap, especially customers who are heavily invested in your company. They think this roadmap will have more details than the sales or executive briefing meetings they typically attend. Customers want to have a say in the direction of the company's products or services and be heard in the CAB meeting. During this roadmap presentation, your executive team will hear why particular features matter for their business and why those features could meet their regulation or industry needs.

When you plan the product or service roadmap, make sure you have product leaders who can speak to the technical features and how they can be applied in a business use case. Often, the roadmap presentation starts on a high level, then dives deeper into what the feature will do. If most of your board customers aren't the "administrators," answer their question(s), but go back to speaking to your entire audience. Additionally, when developing your roadmap be prepared to address the competition, the overall industry, the trends in the industry, and how you've taken all that into consideration in building your roadmap. Even though customers know you've done the leg work, it's often important to share how you've arrived at this roadmap.

At the beginning of the roadmap presentation, include a legal disclaimer about confidentiality. Your legal team or lawyer can provide this disclaimer to you. Mention that everyone in the room has signed a mutual nondisclosure agreement to create a safe environment to share. If you're worried about photos being taken, address this at the beginning of the presentation.

Because the roadmap presentation will generate the most feedback, it's crucial that support staff is present to take notes. With so much information being exchanged, you'll need a notetaker who is observant and knowledgeable, such as a product manager or someone in product marketing. The notetaker should not just transcribe what people say but should also take notes on people's tone and facial cues. For example, you may have an introverted customer who speaks in a calming tone.

A roadmap presentation is typically long. Break it into two sections. The first section can be longer, about forty-five to sixty minutes.

During the presentation, there should be pauses for the board to ask questions. Don't make this a "show-and-tell" of a hundred-plus slides. Substance is more important than abundance. Focus on areas that draw out deeper feedback.

After your first section is over, have a fifteen-minute break and bring in snacks, especially if you served a light lunch. To keep energy levels up, offer protein, like nuts, and some sugar, like sweets, warm cookies, or ice cream in cups as a fun treat.

When starting the second part of the roadmap, don't rush the slides. Pause to ask board customers questions. Don't be surprised if customers want to go back to certain slides to discuss specific topics. Executives and customers may want to ask challenging questions during this part of the presentation. Product owner questions will spark excitement and foster more roadmap discussion.

Why Product Marketing and Product Managers Are Crucial to Developing the CAB Roadmap

When planning the content for your CAB meeting, you'll need both a product manager to create compelling roadmap slides and a product marketing leader to make sure the product is positioned well. The content should also be reviewed by the chief of product or the chief technology officer. Often having another executive review adds a step, but it's important to get it correct. There have been times when CABs had to retract or explain that there's a new name for a particular feature. This shows the CAB team's lack of experience.

Yoav, who has had leadership roles as both a product marketer and a product manager, and I worked on several customer advisory boards together. We spent lots of time debating the best ways to run a CAB, and Yoav is the person who has pushed me the most in my career.

I asked Yoav to share his favorite parts of a CAB meeting.

For me, the CAB highlight is the roadmap. I enjoy watching customers' expressions when they learn of the new features. After many CABs, I believe having the roadmap at the very end is important. If you start a roadmap too early, then the customer board won't feel welcome to advise. They may think, what's the point of doing this now? Do they want us to change their mind? It looks like you're set in your roadmap and want us to just agree.

Yoav also shared his favorite interactive way of engaging with board members during a CAB roadmap session:

When I was a junior product manager, a product leader gave out one hundred dollars of play money. He asked all the customer board members to think through what they would buy from the new roadmap and assigned a price to each feature. Next, he asked the customers to list what they would buy. This experience always created lots of positive excitement, energy, and discussion.

Many boards opt to run a roadmap session and then end the board meeting and move onto cocktails and dinner. If you're running your first CAB, that's a good way to end. However, if you're willing to go the extra mile, it's beneficial to include a business review.

Business Operational Review

Often day two of a CAB event ends with a roadmap session. It's been a long day and people just want to have fun and start to network at the bar. But a CAB requires a significant investment of resources, and your company can get more out of the experience by including a business operational review. While technology is typically the main reason customers purchase a product or service, a business operational review gives the vendor company the opportunity to provide a deep dive into how its departments that directly impact the customers—such as support, quality assurance, resellers, and sales—are functioning. It also gives the company the opportunity to ask its customer advisers for feedback and ideas on how to fix any issues.

For example, a business operational review could focus on poor tier 1 service or offer feedback about junior sales reps. Customer advisers can share their experiences, while the company executives listen and learn. These CAB customer stories help leaders apply resources to fix issues, since customers will describe experiences they want and will often provide solutions. If you're looking to grow your market share or retain your customers, having a business operational review is a must.

How to Select What to Discuss in the Business Operational Review

Your company uses net promoter scores (NPS) or customer satisfaction surveys to measure customer satisfaction. The data can be high level ("Would you recommend us?") or dive deep into a customer's experience with the product, service, and/or employees. Use this data to determine the topics for the business operational review.

Presenting bad news isn't meant to be torture for your executives, but these areas are where executives need the most feedback and candid advice. If the company has already taken steps to address an issue, you can still bring them up in the review and share how you're working toward a solution.

Josh, who was introduced in chapter 1, has this to share on the value of receiving feedback during product and business operational reviews:

> *The cornerstone of the CAB are the product and business feedback sessions, where we can dive deeper into use cases and personas. It's not only group therapy for our customers to share their stories, but for our company leaders, we hear the sticky issues. Often, we've known of those issues, but there's something about being able to put it in the voice of the customer that helps prioritize action.*

Surprisingly, bringing up issues and asking the customer board for advice is the fastest way to build loyalty with your board customers. No one company is perfect. Customers understand that and will find it refreshing that a company is strong and confident enough to ask for feedback. Even customers who have sat on boards have confided in me they wished their company had its own board to ask customers questions. Their company would be better if they did. Remember, though, that listening at the CAB meeting is only one part of building trust and loyalty with customers. Addressing issues and following up after receiving CAB feedback matters a lot to customers.

And don't forget: it's also good to bring up some of the positive feedback from the NPS and survey data too.

Two Ways to Conduct a Business Operational Review

How you conduct your business operational review comes down to communication styles. One way is to have an executive give a presentation to the entire group. The downside of this format is that you'll receive limited feedback. It's more challenging for customers to provide negative feedback in a room full of people. They don't want to be judged, and they will be very careful about what words they use.

Another option is to break out into smaller groups with two executives facilitating the discussion. I've found this format to be the most conducive for sharing negative feedback. It's more relaxed and easier to speak up in a smaller group. In general, people also tend to offer more constructive feedback.

Depending on how you want to structure the smaller groups, you can have several breakouts in rotation. For a CAB with ten customer board members, I suggest three breakout groups (one group will have four customers). Always have one breakout group on the topic of "Other," or whatever is on the minds of customer advisers. It's important to have this general group, because customers may raise new issues that should be addressed. Another reason is that customers are giving a lot of their time to the board, and this breakout session provides them with the opportunity to have company executives address their concerns.

In each breakout group, have two executives and a notetaker. Only the customers will rotate to new breakout sessions. The two executives will be in each session to facilitate, ask questions, and observe. Provide questions for the executives to ask. To develop and compose questions, use your survey data and have your business unit leader help you.

After each breakout is over, ask one of the customers to summarize the feedback. I find that when a customer gives the readout, it's taken more seriously than if an executive does it. It also frees up the executives to sit, listen, and observe customers' physical communication. Head nodding, grins, smiles, and sighs are all communication information.

Rotate the breakouts and try not to have the same customers sit in the same breakout session. Familiarity works, but it's better to get fresh ideas. Additionally, it's a way to help customers network with board peers they haven't had a chance to meet yet. While it's extra work, it increases the overall CAB experience. Often in these breakouts customers confirm what's been a thorn in the side of the business and provide feedback and ideas that can help company executives prioritize solutions and action steps after the board meeting.

After breakfast is a good time to schedule these presentations. They are important but don't need to be allocated as much time as the roadmap and business operational review, which need two to three hours total.

Closing with Acknowledgment

Though the agenda for the day may still include an evening event, it's important to end the second half of the CAB meeting with a closing statement from the CAB executive sponsor, who may be the chief operations officer or the chief product officer. It is important to acknowledge how grateful the company is for the board's time, advice, and constructive feedback, and how the company plans to facilitate follow-up.

Evening Event (Dinner, Experience)

The evening event will likely be the biggest bonding time among the board members. It comes after a full day of learning new information, sharing ideas, and making new connections. The evening event can be planned to have intention. You may want to have your CEO and other executives seated with board members they have specifically asked to sit next to at dinner. Make sure you always place customer board members on both sides of vendor executives. Experiences such as tours of the venue grounds, wine tasting, or live music will heighten the CAB experience and yield more opportunities to bond than just a sit-down for dinner. It's not a must, but it's great to cap off the night with a memorable experience—like the time we opened a giant bottle of champagne with a saber. That experience at golden hour generated spectacular photos that everyone requested copies of as a memento of the occasion.

There are always a few customers who will want to stay up and party. Make sure there's a bar open at the venue and/or have transportation for them if they are going off-site and staying out after the official conclusion of the day's agenda.

Breakfast Meetings (One-on-One Meetings Between Customers and Executives)

After a fun night, plan a full, hot breakfast option to help get everyone going the next day. Many customers and executives like to schedule formal or informal one-on-one meetings during this time. Most seasoned CAB customers will request these meetings. Vendor executives may want to pull a customer aside to ask more follow-up questions. Smaller meetings tend to be positive experiences and show that the board is working, especially when people want to talk to one another and get the maximum value out of the CAB event.

Customer Presentations and New Updates from Other Business Units

During the first full day of the CAB event, 95 percent of the CAB goals should have been met. Day 2 covers what I like to call the "bonus" content, including customer presentations on their deployments and/or new updates from other business units. For example, executives who manage strategic partnerships with other technology or services might present. Hearing from these vendor executives provides a more well-rounded company perspective. If you don't have customer presentations, consider a customer panel.

At the Closing of the CAB Event

The CAB executive sponsor typically gives the closing remarks and should focus on thanking the customers. Additionally, they should include the following reminders:

- The CAB lead will compile the feedback and get back to everyone within twenty-four hours.

- The CAB executive summaries are high level due to the confidentiality of the discussions.

- The customer executive sponsors will set up quarterly calls for the rest of the year.

- The day and time of the follow-up board meeting will be decided.

The sponsor should end by sharing logistical details of any remaining events, such as a closing dinner or experience, and ask the company executives to stay behind for an internal follow-up meeting.

> **Executive Pro Tip:** Don't be afraid to speak up to hold board members accountable.
>
> Having the executive sponsor vocalize how the company will follow up will help hold the company executives accountable.

Internal Executive Follow-Up Meeting

A world-class step in building out your CAB is executives' follow-up. Sadly, most companies with CABs don't have a formal follow-up plan. Put yourself in the shoes of your customers. Imagine you've gone to a wedding (the CAB) and the couple (the executive) doesn't send a thank-you note for the gift you sent them. As an executive, you've put in the work of spending time with your esteemed board. Now it's time to sit down as a team. The internal executive follow-up meeting must happen right after each long day, typically Day 2, and the last day, which is a half day. When the feedback is fresh, the CAB executive sponsor, the COO, or the CPO will lead a meeting. They will go around the room and ask each executive to discuss. This will prompt them to take action. Otherwise, the executive sponsor will assign follow-up, i.e., Mary will follow up with Stuart on his questions about yearly renewals, because she is the chief revenue officer. The follow-up meeting typically takes thirty minutes. You don't want to draw it out, but you have to make sure it's clear the executives are assigned the responsibility to follow up with each customer advisory board member.

The internal executive meeting is the first step in a successful post-CAB program. Chapter 5 covers how to run a post-CAB program in detail and includes best practices and examples of different approaches so you can create your own post-CAB program.

CAB Lead Pro Tip: Always feed your customer advisory board, especially if there was a lot of liquor the night before.

If you have scheduled an evening event with alcoholic refreshments, provide a hot breakfast the next morning to help relieve any hangovers. A half-day CAB event will begin around 11:00 a.m. Be sure to offer a boxed lunch for each member.

Mapping Out Your Final Agenda

To help you finalize your CAB meeting agenda, use a spreadsheet to review the value of each agenda session. This exercise can be done anytime during your CAB planning and can be used to make a solid argument for a heftier budget. This spreadsheet exercise is great for post-CAB too. After your board meeting, it's easier to see if you've achieved your CAB goals and key performance indicators (KPIs). The following page shows figure 4.1, an example of a Mapping CAB Goals to the Agenda spreadsheet. This can also be viewed at **www.ireneyam.com/cabresources_mapcabgoals** or scan the QR code to take you to the template site.

Figure 4.1: Mapping CAB Goals to the Agenda

Topic (est. time)	Speaker	Value for Customer	Goals and Soft (S) or Hard (H) KPI	Benefits for Company	Other
Opening, Welcome (10 minutes)/ Icebreaker activity (30–40 minutes)	Company executive sponsor	Review the agenda and add specific details or highlights of each session.	G: Everyone is on the same page and has an activity to open people up to feel safe to share.	Sets the tone of the CAB.	Review any housekeeping actions.
Company overview (15–30 minutes)	CEO	Get VIP access to the company's goals.	G: Share reasons why they are having a CAB. S: Trust	Get validation.	Create a space to be vulnerable.
New Help Desk Platform Discussion Point 1 (45 minutes: 30 minutes for presentation and 15 minutes for discussion)	CCO	View demo for the first time.	G: Start with an easy issue to get customers to open up. S: Trust, advice, building confidence in brand.	Get feedback.	
Break (10–15 minutes)		Private conversations and bonding over ideas.	G: Build bonds with customers S: Trust		
New Strategy Discussion Point 2 (45 minutes: 30 minutes for presentation and 15 minutes for discussion)	CTO (Have 3–4 C-suite executives on the panel.)	Learn new areas of research and development.	G: Executives have questions and need customer insight and validation. S: Trust, advice H: Increase company outlook, leads to increase in sales cycle	Being open to answering questions.	Board customers often have the same issues or concerns. Talking about them acts as group therapy and fosters bonds.

Session	Owner	Description	Objectives		Notes
Lunch (45–60 minutes) (The time depends on the rest of the day's schedule.)		Network with executives and fellow customers.	G: More focus with customers who executives are interested in forming a relationship with. S: Networking, peer intellect H: CAB customers sharing their experiences becomes a real-time customer testimonial that could spark new purchases from other customers on the board.	Executives get placed next to customers they want to build a relationship with.	
Customer Keynote: How we increase productivity Q&A (10 minutes keynote and 10 minutes for Q&A)	CAB customer, a VP of IT	Customers learn new practices on how to increase productivity from a peer.	G: To excite other customers on how to use their product in a different way. S: Customer advocacy H: Upsell	Board customers who deployed a full suite within 18 months.	The customer shares how they created professional services training for regional managers.
Roadmap: focus on key features, not all features (45–60 minutes for presentation; 30 minutes for discussion)	CPO	Get an overview of the roadmap and provide input.	G: Customer input on roadmap. Are we innovative? Will customers be confident in our technology? S: Networking, peer intellect H: Upsell by peers	Gather insights from decision-makers; what's compelling for the decision-maker persona.	Customers often will bring up their experiences here, both positive and negative.

Figure 4.1: *Continued*

Topic (est. time)	Speaker	Value for Customer	Goals and Soft (S) or Hard (H) KPI	Benefits for Company	Other
Break (10–15 minutes)		Time to pull people aside for a private conversation.	G: Bonding with customers S: Trust		
Business Operational Review Breakouts 1. Support 2. Professional Services 3. New Pricing (40 minutes each review: 15 minutes for discussion of topic and need to summarize; 5 minutes per group to present the summary, discussion; 20 minutes to open up for cross-group discussion/questions)	Facilitators and customer board members.	Build peer support. Discuss non-customer, topical issues that board members can take back to their own businesses. Share practices.	G: Review areas of the business that need improvement, hear firsthand from customers what they want. S: Trust	1. Learn what customers think of your support. 2. Learn what professional services engagement is like. 3. Gather customer concerns with the new pricing.	Break out into groups to create new one-on-one connections.

Additional Breakout Topics: about workforce/ economy 1. Transitioning back to the office (Are employees coming back to the office? What's working, what's not working?) 2. Economy outlook—recession (A recession may be coming. How do we adjust our budgets but keep innovating?) (40 minutes each review: 15 minutes for discussion of topic and need to summarize; 5 minutes per group to present the summary, discussion; 20 minutes to open up for cross-group discussion/ questions.	Facilitators, COO, and customer board member	Other non-customer issues, but topical issues for the board to gather input from other board members. How other peers solve these issues.	G: Listening to how the customers solve other challenges. S: Fostering rapport and support for the customer	1. Gather best practices. 2. Gauge if customers are tightening their budgets in 2024 and where they will spend their dollars. (helps with company forecast sales).	Learn more of each customer's company and their culture.

Figure 4.1: *Continued*

Topic (est. time)	Speaker	Value for Customer	Goals and Soft (S) or Hard (H) KPI	Benefits for Company	Other
Closing with Acknowledgment: Explain Executive Sponsorship Program (10–15 minutes) Spend more time explaining the executive sponsorship program.	CAB lead or company executive sponsor	Customer board benefits	G: Be clear about the CAB program's next steps. S: Trust	Keep the conversation going and deepen connections between company executives and customer advisory board members.	Read the room for CAB sentiment. Gauge whether customers look satisfied with the CAB. Are they peppy or do they have a drained look?
Internal Executive Follow-Up (30 minutes)	Discuss pending issues. Make sure the vendor executive is clear who is following up and taking action from the requests.	Vendor benefit	G: Learn from any private conversations with the CAB customer(s).	Clear communication between vendor executives and who will take responsibility.	Important to have if the vendor team is new and doesn't have experience in being part of a CAB.
Happy Hour and Dinner (45–60 minutes for Happy Hour; 60 minutes for dinner)		Relax and have more time to meet one another, develop deeper relationships.	G: Building relationships, asking direct questions. S: Network H: Upsell and cross-sell	Ask candid questions one-on-one with customers.	Build rapport and comfort with peers. The shy people may open up at cocktail/dinnertime.

Session	Owner	Customer benefit	Goals	Vendor benefit	Notes
Breakfast Meetings (one-on-one meeting with executives) (30-45 minutes; you could have two 20-minute meetings, 5 minutes to move around, get more coffee)		Access to executives before having to travel home.	G: Provides one-on-one time S: Network, trust	Provides one-on-one time, especially after all the information shared, and receives more honest feedback.	
Customer Presentations, new updates from other business units (10–15 minutes for presentations and 10 minutes for Q&A)	VP of Strategy or VP of Partnerships	Learning of new partnerships that the customers leverage.	G: Confirm that the company strategy is solid. Gather feedback on how they feel about the company's brand. S: Trust H: May consider investing more in CAB company.	Provides access to customers that could help develop more strategic partnerships.	
Closing of the CAB Event CAB adjourned to make afternoon flights (10–15 minutes)	Company executive sponsor	Confirmation of next steps, what the vendor is committed to doing going forward.	G: Communications and how the company plans to run their CAB program S: Trust	Openly sharing, helps with keeping all the vendor CAB executives accountable.	
Must: Internal Executive Follow-Up (30 minutes)	Executive Sponsor: Discuss pending issues. Make sure the vendor executives are clear who is following up and taking action on the requests.	Vendor benefits	G: Gather all the feedback and follow up with customers.	Clear communication between vendor executives and who will take responsibility.	A must meeting for the executive team.

How Much Time to Allot for Each Session

After you've built your agenda, give yourself a high five. It's a feat in itself! But there's still more to do. Now you'll need to allot an amount of time for each session of the CAB event. Session times aren't precise like a Swiss watch, but you'll want to make sure you get through all the sessions to meet your CAB goals.

Keeping to the schedule is often the hardest part of running a CAB event. The CAB lead may have to announce a change in the agenda, perhaps shortening lunches from sixty minutes to forty minutes to make sure there is enough time for the afternoon sessions.

> **CAB Lead Pro Tip:** Include time buffers to your sessions.
>
> For example, during a full day of scheduled meetings, add a 15-minute buffer to the morning session and a 15-minute buffer to the afternoon session. This way, you only have to start worrying about compromising the day's schedule if meetings veer more than 15 minutes off track. If that happens, either the CAB lead or the company executive sponsor should let the board know they need to table the discussion and/or park the ideas in order to continue with the CAB agenda.
>
> *If the conversation is heated, don't stop it. Let it finish. Then communicate the need to move on to the next agenda topic.*

The amount of time you decide to allot for each session will be unique to your company's needs. I've included one example of how to allocate time for a CAB agenda on page 111. In general, I recommend:

Company Overview: 35 minutes

I find this is an adequate amount of time for executives to deliver a well-rounded update. (This is not supposed to be a quick snapshot!) I encourage executives to be real with customer board members and share information they would provide their board of directors. They should show some vulnerability and be honest but not flashy.

CAB Discussion Points: About 1 hour

It's important to give executives and customers sufficient time for discussion, and especially for customers to share feedback and ideas. Executives should pose succinct questions to customers (for example, when do you hire professional services and why?) and allow time for customers to ask questions in return. These sessions are important, but don't extend the time allotted too much and take away from other components of the CAB event.

Roadmap: No more than 2 hours

This is often considered the main event and, given the amount of information executives need to share for it to be meaningful, it may be the longest session of the CAB meeting. That said, while a product roadmap is an essential component, so is listening to the customer share their thoughts during the CAB discussion point sessions. Learning how your customers think and what their challenges are provides the kind of insight that will let you know if your customers will deploy the new product features highlighted on the roadmap. Keeping the roadmap session short or providing a midpoint break or fun activity maintains focus and allows adequate time to gather feedback from your board members.

Breakout Sessions: 10–60 minutes

If you plan on having multiple sessions, it can be a little nerve-wracking for the customers (they go from sitting in a large room to smaller groups where they are expected to participate). Provide a 10 minute-break between sessions and make sure you have delicious sugary snacks—fruit works—to keep people energized. However, if the board is deep in discussions, sticking to the agenda isn't wise. For example, the company CFO wants to explore whether the customer would pay more for your product/service. Having a longer breakout, providing time for people on the board to connect, will foster more connection and trust.

One of the most challenging components to schedule are the two discussion point sessions on Day 2. Not all discussions are equal. Discussion 1 can take longer than 2 and vice versa. Planning enough time for each discussion depends on the following:

- Are you presenting something on which the board will provide constructive feedback? If yes, how elaborate is the topic and are you looking for every CAB member to give you feedback?

- How many questions do you have for your customer board members to engage in deeper feedback or advice?

It's best to minimize the presentation slides during discussions. Try to engage with three slides. Typically, an executive has a strategy, and they may present this strategy in a slide, then ask customers for their input. Encourage the speaker to present for 7 to 10 minutes. Note, you'll likely only get 60 to 70 percent of the board to comment. Give each customer about 5 minutes for their input. This total discussion will likely take 40 to 60 minutes. If you are planning to reveal or share a solution, present it after a few customers share. Often, you'll see a before-and-after response, and that can help with your positioning and strategic future planning. If the discussion is cut short, the notetaker will make a note to follow up.

In each discussion, there should be four internal roles: speaker, facilitator, observer, and notetaker. You may be surprised that there's an observer role, but it's important to have. Often board members may be unsure what to say or they can't find the words, but their bodies may give the board feedback—such as a grin, a smile, crossed arms, or darting eyes. The observer's role is to write this down. This may later lead to a follow-up private conversation or provide informational data.

A good rule of thumb is to give each discussion a minimum of 20 to 30 minutes. Let the facilitator know that they must be the one to keep the customers on the board engaged. Ask your executives to play the part of facilitators by having them listen intently and asking customer board members questions. Have the notetaker keep time and have them provide a 10-minute and then a 5-minute signal to wrap it up. When wrapping up, make sure to train the facilitator to be sincere, not abrupt. This is often challenging, because they're under pressure to move on to the next topic.

It's not uncommon for a CAB agenda to change two or three times during the planning stage. You and your company executive sponsor will spend the most planning time figuring out the agenda and the time allotment for each session. Here's an example of how you could allot time for a three-day/two-night CAB agenda.

3-Day In-Person CAB Agenda Time Allotment

*** Day 1 ***

Afternoon Arrival

4:30–8:00 p.m.: Evening Kickoff Cocktails (drinks and small bites for people to network)

5:00 p.m.: Welcome/Icebreaker Activity (30–40 minutes)

*** Day 2 ***

6:30–8:00 a.m.: Breakfast

8:00–8:10 a.m.: Morning: Opening of the CAB & Welcome

8:10–8:45 a.m.: Company Overview (In-Depth)

8:45–9:45 a.m.: CAB Discussion Point 1

9:45–10:00 a.m.: Midmorning Break

10:00–11:15 a.m.: CAB Discussion Point 2

11:15–12:15 p.m.: Lunch

12:15–12:45 p.m.: Customer Guest Speaker

12:45–2:00 p.m.: Product or Service Roadmap Part 1

2:00–2:15 p.m.: Midafternoon Break

2:15–3:30 p.m.: Product or Service Roadmap Part 2

3:30–4:00 p.m.: Business Operational Review

4:00–4:30 p.m.: Breakouts

4:30–5:15 p.m.: Closing CAB with Acknowledgment

5:30–8:30 p.m.: Evening Event (Dinner, Experience)

*** Day 3 ***

7:30–9:00 a.m.: Breakfast Meetings (one-on-one meeting with executives)

9:00–10:45 a.m.: Customer Presentations, new updates from other business units

10:45–11:00 a.m.: CAB adjourned to make afternoon flights

11:00–12:00 p.m.: CAB Internal Executive Follow-Up Meeting

Chapter 4 covered the following:

- Standard elements of a CAB agenda, including the opening, presentations, discussions, breaks, and closing.

- The importance of choosing effective speakers.

- What you can present or discuss during each agenda item to best achieve your company's goals.

- How to map out and allot time for your own CAB agenda.

Even with the perfect agenda, CABs don't always go as planned. An angry customer can throw off the balance of the energy in the room. But there are ways to mitigate damage. In the next chapter, you will learn how to address problems that may happen during a CAB.

5
TROUBLESHOOTING WHEN AN IN-PERSON CAB PLAN GOES SIDEWAYS

You've poured a hundred hours of work into planning the CAB event. You're ready to enjoy the CAB and focus on providing the best experience for your customers and your executives. And then you're thrown a curveball that could upend all your carefully laid plans: a slashed budget, significantly expanded goals, an irate or tuned-out customer board member, a CAB meeting crasher. In this chapter, I'll share strategies for troubleshooting some of the most common issues that arise before the CAB meeting kickoff and during the event. Staying calm and focused on solutions is key.

CAB Case Study: CAB Budget Reimagined

This case study describes the most challenging CAB experience I've ever had—and my all-time favorite CAB experience because I learned how to be more flexible. I hope it shows you how you can stay resilient through unexpected and last-minute changes to the agenda and still build a world-class CAB experience for yourself, your customers, and your executives.

Background

The company I was working for just had an IPO and finally had global reach and brand recognition. It had also started to beat the better-known network appliance companies. I was ready to take on a new challenge and elevate our CAB program by hosting customers from global brands around the world. My big budget was approved, and I started to envision a fancy CAB meeting at a winery in Napa, California.

Early in the planning stage, I was called into a meeting with several other colleagues and told we would be acquiring a small start-up. I didn't think much of it, until a senior product marketing colleague, who was now the main product lead for the newly acquired start-up, asked me to run two CABs simultaneously to appeal to two distinct sets of customers: those for our flagship product (IT or network directors) and those for the start-up we acquired (IT or network engineers). To keep our nimble competitive edge, we wanted to achieve two nontraditional goals with these CABs. One goal was to seek feedback from both CABs by asking each customer how we should market our solutions jointly, since now we were widening our buyer persona to include network engineers. The second goal was to upsell our products.

Executives liked the idea of two CABs running simultaneously and thought it would impress investors and the market, something they were very eager to do. I was against it. I feel strongly that CAB events should not be upselling events. As a CAB lead, I wanted to create experiences so global brand customers could spend more time with our executives and product leaders. The new mandate concerned me, but there was no time for a debate. Instead, I focused on finding a solution.

My solution was to find common ground between the two CAB agendas. I first focused on CAB networking events for the two board meetings. Then I reworked the agendas until I found what I felt would be a win-win-win for the executives, customers, and CAB program.

Solution

Due to the acquisition, the marketing budgets were cut. I had to get creative, so that meant no fancy Napa CAB experience. I was able to get the budget increased by 20 percent since I would be hosting twenty customers instead of ten. Hosting meant I had to budget flights and hotel rooms for the customer board members. With this budget, I could only host them for a day and the following morning.

I decided to have the CAB meeting at the company headquarters (HQ) in San Francisco. Our corporate travel expert had secured a corporate rate at a large chain hotel, and it became the CAB headquarters hotel because it was the shortest walking distance to HQ. Having the CAB meeting at the company headquarters presented new challenges, so I asked our facilities team, the office manager, and the office receptionist to help plan and execute the event.

Venue Challenges

The company's office space was cozy. It was mostly open space and didn't have a lot of meeting rooms. However, it did have big kitchens. It also didn't have a cafeteria, since it was right in the heart of South of Market in San Francisco. I decided to make the cozy headquarters an experience for our board members.

Welcoming Our Board

When customers arrived on the morning of the first day, they were given a tour of the office. Our office manager and receptionist pitched in to give tours since we would have staggered groups. The tours gave customers an inside look at how we worked together, even showing that our cofounder and CEO sat in an open cube just like everyone else (except for the chief financial officer and head of human resources, who had their own offices).

After the tour, I organized a catered breakfast in the engineering break room. I selected the engineering break room because it had the most toys: Ping-Pong, pool, foosball, video game consoles, big flat-screen TVs, and an Italian espresso machine.

What made the company special was that engineering and product managers really spent time with customers. So, during the breakfast—a networking part of the CAB event—I wanted the customer board members to network with one another and meet the engineers and support staff whom they had talked to but never had a chance to meet in person. As part of the CAB meeting planning process, I had asked the product managers to invite engineers and support staff who were located in our San Francisco offices to the breakfast to meet the customer board members. The result was a hugely positive experience filled with a lot of buzz and excitement. The newly acquired customer board members felt welcomed, and it was easy for people to mingle. The breakfast really helped break the ice before we all sat down for the meetings.

Bringing Both CAB Audiences Together for the Company Overview

I pitched the idea of having the cofounder and CEO present one Company Overview to both audiences. The CEO agreed, and it was easier for him to prepare one presentation. The CEO stated the CAB mission and explained why we were hosting two CABs. The CEO openly shared undisclosed news of two new global strategic partnerships and thanked the boards for helping establish us as a world-class network hardware and software company.

Running Two Roadmap Presentations Simultaneously

After the company's insider overview, we asked the customers to join the CAB roadmap they were invited to.

This was an agenda shift I advocated for. Usually, we would move from the company overview into the two discussion sessions with the product roadmap discussion after lunch, but I decided to have the morning CAB meetings focus on the product roadmap because I wanted the afternoon to be free for both CAB audiences to move freely and feel invited to learn more about the other products from the CAB board members.

This schedule was frowned upon by our product management team because their preference is to have the entire afternoon to walk through their entire roadmap. I countered that if they wanted customers to give product feedback about their roadmap, then non-customers of that product who sat through the roadmap wouldn't be the right audience to provide real customer examples for feedback.

I challenged product managers to focus on specific features that would have crossover interests and themes. These crossover topics would first engage customer board members to speak. Because each board member knew their use cases well, the afternoon breakouts would help us meet our objective of learning how both customer board personas would speak to both products. That is, how would they describe this as a network solution. We wanted our customers to tell us in their words how they would describe our products.

The midmorning roadmap presentations worked well, and since they were held at our headquarters, the vice presidents of engineering sat in on the roadmap meetings to hear opinions about the features, and the product marketer from both products took notes and wrote down observations.

> **CAB Lead and Executive Pro Tip:** Observations and Body Language
>
> All CAB sessions should have notetakers to take down what customers and executives say. Notetakers must also jot down audience reactions—that is, when people smiled, smirked, frowned, folded their hands, etc.— during a presentation or discussion. Not everyone speaks up, but they do communicate with body language. Jotting down these important observations will provide more data for the product managers and executives to review and reflect on after the CAB meeting.

Lunch Was Together

The company HQ was next to a rustic-chic California restaurant, perfect for our CAB lunch. We had a long table in a cozy room, and even a VIP entrance that made our customers feel very special. To help the customers get the most out of conversations, the table seating chart consisted of an experienced board member seated next to a new network monitoring board member who was a network engineer, and in every third seat, I placed a company executive.

Before the CAB, I asked the executives to do more listening and less talking at lunch. It was more important to allow the two different CAB board members to network, connect, and hopefully find commonality among themselves than it was to talk about our company.

Often coffee is served with dessert. However, I opted not to include coffee when it was dessert time to prevent board members and executives from lingering at the restaurant. As the dessert was being passed around, I reviewed the afternoon agenda. I brought up housekeeping items, such as that coffee, tea, and extra snacks would be provided in each meeting room. I emphasized coffee to get the board back into the meetings. I also reminded them of our happy hour at 5:00 p.m. I handed out a printout of the afternoon CAB sessions and encouraged board members to move freely between sessions.

> **CAB Lead Pro Tip:** Afternoon session setup
>
> Place coffee and tea service inside the meeting room to keep the board meeting moving. If you set it up outside the meeting room, board members will linger there.

Afternoon Sessions

I designed the afternoon with two simultaneous forty-five-minute product-focused sessions and provided every CAB member with the agenda ahead of time, so they could decide which session they wanted to join before arriving in San Francisco. Because a goal of the CABs was to find messaging and positioning for both products that would resonate with two buying personas, I suggested the product marketers spend the first five minutes of each session explaining the features to everyone, so current customers and non-customers could be on the same page. Then I asked them to focus on the benefits of the features. For example, how the features can reduce mean time to repair networks, reduce downtime, and resolve network issues. Because we had recently bought the new start-up, we wanted to test our product messaging and positioning with the two different CAB groups to help us understand what resonated with each board member.

During these sessions, I asked our leaders to leave their egos at the door and to be honest and vulnerable. I also asked for each CAB member's help in positioning the products in the marketplace. The outcome was a flood of ideas. The members discussed what technical terms to use and what not to use, what terms they would search for in a web browser, and when product terms sounded like "marketing." The discussion made everyone chuckle and grin. It was fun and it also built camaraderie. The board members enjoyed being advisers.

Due to the budget, this became a product-centric CAB. We didn't have the budget to host a second day to go into support, professional services, or customer experience.

CAB Lead Pro Tip: Ensuring a high-quality conference experience in a nontraditional meeting venue.

Since the CAB event was being held in our headquarters—a place of business—instead of a traditional meeting venue, I stationed a CAB concierge person outside each meeting room. We offered board members a VIP experience by serving them drinks and showing them where they could take a private call or the location of the restrooms. This took a great deal of intercompany cooperation with the office and facilities management team and was vital to the success of the CABs.

Closing the CABs

We closed both CAB meetings by asking board members if this format worked for them. Many customers said the format was unique, but they understood the reason. They wished they could have had at least another half day to spend more time with the entire board to review other parts of our business. I took this feedback as a big win. If customers shared that they wanted more time with us, then that shows we created a world-class experience.

CAB Lead Pro Tip: Ask all the board members if they are willing to share their network and contact information immediately after the CAB meeting.

Don't assume that everyone is willing to be contacted. Ask them when the excitement of the event is fresh and use the opportunity to gauge whether the CAB was a success by observing people's body language. People smiling and nodding enthusiastically to share means they really enjoyed themselves and sincerely want to connect after the in-person meeting. Customers who don't want to connect tend to look down or grin with a pensive expression.

I asked the notetakers to meet with me before we headed into Happy Hour, and I also asked the head of every product to join us. Luckily, we had no one who needed a private one-on-one meeting and no escalations. There were some customers asking for product follow-ups and demos for their team. I asked the engineers who attended breakfast to attend the Happy Hour with the board members.

Wrapping It Up

Because of our budget, we hosted a Happy Hour instead of a dinner to wrap up the CAB. We provided plenty of food and windbreakers due to San Francisco's unpredictable late-summer weather. We rented a frozen margarita machine and served cold Coronas with plenty of ripe limes, old-fashioned soda in glass bottles, and delicious local tacos from the Mission District. After the Happy Hour, many of the board members went out in smaller groups, while others had plans with their friends or family in San Francisco.

The next morning was the informal closing of the CAB. This was intentional. I knew that we would have customers who wanted time with our teams. Most of the board members rented their own cars to maximize their time in the San Francisco Bay Area/Silicon Valley to meet with their other vendors for executive briefing meetings.

After the CAB

The company saw the following outcomes from the CABs:

No Need for Executive Follow-Ups or a Formal CAB Executive Sponsored Program

Note, before we had the two CABs we made the conscious decision not to offer a traditional post-CAB executive program where executives would follow up. Our salespeople already did a phenomenal job escalating issues and asking executives to join customer meetings. I made sure the product management and marketing leaders followed up with sales to prioritize demo requests and offered to help executives who needed help setting up one-on-one CAB customer meeting requests.

Benefits of Running Two CABs Simultaneously

- Ninety percent of the flagship product CAB members bought the new network monitoring product within six weeks. This was a big win in the eyes of the leadership, especially because of the timing of the CAB meeting: it made our end-of-year numbers glow green.

- Fifty percent of the network monitoring CAB members purchased the flagship solution. The rest of the CAB customers passed along what they learned to their VP of IT or the CIO. I saw this as a positive because we had access through introductions made by board members to new IT decision-makers who would take our meetings.

- Product management and product marketing received excellent feedback on how to position products and show customers the problems they solve. We also passed key words and terms to our search optimization team. This, in turn, helped us rebuild our sales training and marketing content, and it helped on search strategies.

Executive Pro Tip: Give kudos to everyone who worked on the CAB.

Post-CAB meeting, the CAB executive sponsor should always thank everyone at the company who worked on the CAB in an internal newsletter or during an all-hands meeting.

Following Year, Two Separate CABs

Since the two-CAB format worked for us, we hosted two CABs the following year, adding an additional day for more roadmap learnings and discussions.

Many from the CAB flagship product wanted to discuss professional services and support issues in Asia and Europe. The company was shifting into a global enterprise company, and our customers wanted to advise on areas that needed attention, because they were used to the level of service offered by other mature billion-dollar technology companies in Asia and Europe. After the second year, we decided to split up and have two individual CABs.

CAB Solutions: When CABs Go Sideways

Over the course of my career, I have only had a handful of board meetings go sideways. If you find yourself dealing with an upset or unfocused CAB member or a CAB meeting crasher, I hope the way I handled these situations will help you. Above all, do your best to stay calm and avoid becoming emotional in front of customers.

Handling an Upset CAB Member
Right Before the CAB Meeting

Two days before the CAB meeting, a customer account sales rep contacted me. They were concerned that a state agency board member would be upset because their data center was currently experiencing outages. Sales had already escalated their issues to support. They had the heads of product and data center experts on calls with the field engineers to fix the issues. Everything that could be done was being done, but the rep wanted to prepare me in case the customer was upset.

My mind was racing: How should we deal with a possibly explosive customer at the CAB meeting? Would the customer lash out and send the CAB into a negative spiral? I dug into my notes for his details, called him, and went to his voicemail. I left a message apologizing for his data center being down, and I asked to talk to him about the CAB and how I could help.

To my surprise, he called me back within twenty-four hours. He was understandably frustrated, and I didn't take his tone personally. He still wanted to fly out for the CAB. As a state government agency employee, he paid for his own flight and hotel. Next, I sprinted down the office hallway and almost barged my way into the general manager's door. The GM wasn't there. An hour later, I found him.

The Solution

The GM was seasoned and calm. I suggested that I get his executive administrator to change his flight so he could meet with the customer one-to-one before the CAB meeting kickoff. The GM and the CAB customer agreed to meet privately before the CAB meeting started in the morning, and they met for a nightcap. I didn't get to find out what happened, but during the next morning's sessions, the customer was quiet, keeping to himself, and preoccupied.

I took it upon myself to be more attentive to the upset customer. As I walked by him, I smelled smoke on his blazer. I asked a company executive who smoked to engage with him on smoke breaks. The executive learned there were multiple issues with their data center.

When I heard that, I pulled the customer aside and asked if he needed any additional help. He shared that the GM had already requested not only the field team, but regional experts to stay in the customer's data center until it was back up. Later that day, the CAB customer started to relax and engage during the roadmap and demo discussions. We learned later that right before the roadmap the customer's data center was back up and running.

Toward the end of the day, I pulled him aside to apologize and thank him for attending our CAB meeting even though his data center was down. He read between the lines that I was grateful that he hadn't lashed out. He said that having timely access to the GM and talking with the executive during the smoke breaks quelled his anger and nerves. He felt supported even though his data center was down and thanked me for checking in on him.

When the yearly maintenance and upgrades rolled around, this CAB customer didn't hesitate to renew. He asked to be upgraded from Gold to Platinum support. The GM was the customer's advocate. He worked with the sales VP to give the state agency customer a special discount on Platinum support. When the customer found out, he was overjoyed.

With state budget cuts, this state agency customer still continued to invest in our storage solutions and decided to buy all tiers of storage with us because of how we had supported the data center outage.

The personal connections we make can turn a very irate customer into a happier customer. The CAB meeting setting, access to the GM, the army of resources we called upon, and meeting the product and engineering leaders helped the customer feel more confident about his investment during the data center downtime. As a result, he grew close to the GM, who is now just a text away. I learned later that they would share and discuss features and trends by texting and hopping on calls.

When the CAB Customer Isn't Focused

During another CAB, I had one open CAB spot, so I decided to ask a dynamic sales rep who had never nominated his customer for CAB if he wanted to nominate one of his marquee customers. He told me he had a brilliant network architect from London who would be fantastic on our board. The architect also worked for a global IT database company that had a lot of cachet at the time. I didn't have the extra budget to fly this customer in, so I asked for an exception. Our CFO approved the request, and because this customer was from one of the most well-known database vendors in the world, upgraded his flight to business class. Before the CAB, I asked numerous times for a pre-CAB call, but the customer didn't show up for a meeting twice. The sales rep told me there was nothing to worry about and to write all the pre-CAB information in an email, because this customer often worked in the middle of the night.

At the CAB meeting, I placed him in a prominent seat near our CEO. However, the customer was the opposite of brilliant, or maybe he was too brilliant, because he sat through the meetings and wasn't engaged. I kicked myself for not trying harder to have a pre-CAB meeting with him. I finally had the guts to pull him aside at a break. I asked if he needed anything and if he was interested in the presentations. He said, "No, the presentations were informative. I'm just jet-lagged." During lunch, I asked our receptionist to get a couple of cans of Red Bull. As customers were finishing up their lunch, I went alongside the customer's chair and offered him a Red Bull or espresso in the afternoon. He picked the Red Bull. He finally perked up and provided roadmap feedback. He brought up the new UK privacy laws and suggested we talk to his lead engineer after the CAB meeting.

The Solution

Always check in with the customer. If you have people from overseas joining your CAB, have a couple four-packs of Red Bull and espressos handy for jet-lagged customers.

The CAB Crasher

It's not unheard of for an executive to book their own travel and hotel and crash the CAB meeting. This has happened to me. A sales engineer executive unexpectedly arrived at the morning session, I reminded him we had planned the meeting with a strict one-to-one ratio and that the executives in the room had joined the executive sponsorship program and accepted a yearlong responsibility to be a point of contact for their customer post-CAB. Then, I gave him an agenda and created a space for him.

The Solution

If an uninvited executive shows up, guide the crasher to a seat in the back. Or if there's space in the meeting room, add them to the table. Ask your company executive sponsor to make a quick introduction, explaining what value the newcomer brings to the board. Later, have the company executive sponsor have a one-on-one talk with the CAB crasher to determine the best way to move forward.

If you anticipate an executive showing up uninvited and know in your gut it would be difficult to speak to the CAB crasher at the meeting, prepare a contingency plan with your company executive sponsor before the start of the CAB event. When the crasher joins the board meeting, the company executive sponsor can incorporate them into the proceedings while you do the behind-the-scenes work to add another person to the meeting, meals, and activities.

Even CABs that have unexpected events can turn out really well.

Chapter 5 covered the following:

- What to do if you have an angry customer, and how to turn them into an advocate.
- How to increase engagement from jet-lagged customers.
- What you should do in the event of a CAB crasher.

Your work isn't done when the CAB meeting wraps up. Following up with customers is what seals the deal for maintaining long-term relationships. In the next chapter, you will learn how to create a world-class post-CAB program.

6
EXECUTING A WORLD-CLASS POST-CAB PROGRAM

The best CAB event is like a bowl of piping hot wontons with egg noodles (or your favorite home-cooked meal): deeply satisfying and so wonderful you don't want it to end. The measure of a CAB meeting's success is the connections that are made from the conversations between executives and customers—and you want to maintain those connections.

I believe it's the post-CAB meeting connections between executives and peers that continue to create even more career and personal memories.

This chapter is focused on internal and external CAB communication. It's crucial to build out a post-CAB communication plan to continue to connect with your customer board members. A CAB survey is often used to close out the communications between the customers and executives. While that's one simple way to close the loop, in this chapter, you'll learn a long-term strategy that yields the most from your time with your customer advisers.

What to Do Right After the CAB

Celebrate

First and foremost, do some high fives and celebrate your team's achievement. Hosting a CAB event is a twenty-four-hour job, and the team must "be on" at all times. It's exhausting on every level. Thank everyone on the team. Please don't skip this step.

Self-Reflect and Capture Your Thoughts

As soon as you can, take a moment to jot down any thoughts on the CAB and notes on who needs follow-up. After a few hours, those little details are often forgotten. I typically take about ten minutes to write it all down.

Capture Feedback as a Team

Gather all the internal CAB company leaders to attend the Internal Executive Follow-Up Meeting. This is best done immediately after the close of the CAB event. Ask the notetaker to take notes during this review. The company executive sponsor will lead the meeting by using the CAB agenda to assign actions and follow-ups.

Executive Pro Tip: Always check with the notetaker for any extra details.

Have the company executive sponsor ask the notetaker if they've missed any actions that need to be taken.

The company executive sponsor will ask each internal leader who attends the CAB meeting to take responsibility for action items and work with their teams to follow-up with the customer. Note that the leader may need to have several calls with the CAB customer and their team to get to the bottom of an issue or concern. This is the right thing to do, and these interactions will reinforce trust between you and your customers.

Update Post-CAB Customer Dashboard/Profiles with Confirmed CAB Sponsor

Often after the CAB meeting, executives want to switch the customer they have been assigned to sponsor with another executive's customer. Sometimes executives just hit it off with a different customer. You may need to change a customer's CAB Sponsor and update the CAB Customer Dashboard/Profiles. See the last column in the example below.

Post-CAB Customer Dashboard/Profiles

Name	Ron Peni
Title	CIO
Email	rp@xp.com
Company/ Industry	XP/ Consulting
Product in use	1, 2, 3, 4
Professional services	Yes, for custom onboarding
Current sales opportunities	Stage 4: three more products of 1
Support tickets?	Yes, tier 1 (days open 2)
Rep/CSM/ PS	Kim P./ Mike M./Gary S.
Global?	Brazil and Japan
Partner	IBM
CAB Sponsor (previous) If there's a change, list the previous sponsor*	James: CIO Change to Bella: SVP of PS

Post-CAB Meeting Executive Summary for Customer Board Members

The long-lasting value of a CAB meeting is determined by how well company executives follow up with customers. In my experience, sharing a high-level summary of CAB discussions is crucial. I email an executive summary within forty-eight hours after the conclusion of the CAB meeting.

To help me get this done on deadline, I create an executive summary template in a presentation slide format using the CAB branding and design before the start of the CAB event. The template saves time on overall formatting, and I can just focus on the content and copy.

Components of a Post-CAB Meeting Executive Summary

- High-level feedback and the executive taking responsibility

Example: The professional services team should offer additional on-site technical consultants for three days to three months. The SVP of professional services is responsible for overseeing this.

- How issues will be addressed

Example: One to two weeks after the initial CAB meeting, offer a CAB update over a video conference to report on the change, addition, or fix, and drill down to the next steps.

- Communications of "no"

This is often a tough thing to convey in a summary. There are two ways to handle it: either have a one-to-one meeting between the CAB sponsor and the customer or be transparent with the board.

Example: We looked into adding X features, but given our limited resources right now, we won't be able to build it. It's flagged in our project log, which is reviewed regularly, as a CAB consideration.

- Additional components of the executive summary:

  o Discussions and actions being taken, who's the internal owner (VP or executive), and next steps

  o Customer logos of those who attended the CAB

  o CAB photos to share memories

- A thank-you note from the CEO or the company executive sponsor of the board

There are customer board members who have shared details of their business or industry. Never assume they want those details out in public. In other words, be careful and discreet in how you communicate the feedback from a CAB meeting. CAB discussions are confidential; explicitly remind the board about the CAB confidentiality agreement they signed.

CAB Lead Pro Tip: Provide a CAB Executive Summary within forty-eight hours.

This is important because it shows the customers were heard as advisers. It also shows what actions you're taking as a company.

Internal Sign-Off of the CAB Executive Summary

Ensure your company executive sponsor will review the executive summary in a presentation format before you send it out—remember, you'll be sending it to CAB members within forty-eight hours. Have a prewritten thank-you message ready and get the company executive sponsor's approval of the draft ahead of time. Right after the CAB, update the draft to include any specific details, then get the final thank-you message signed off on by your company executive sponsor.

When you send out this summary to your CAB customer, introduce their appointed CAB sponsor and copy the CAB sponsor for their first one-on-one call.

Encourage your CAB customers to present the CAB executive summary to their executives or skip-level employees. Remind the customers when presenting the report to add their CAB experience to round out the briefing to their leadership.

The executive summary is meant to share insights from the CAB and to make sure your customer board members have something tangible to share with their leaders. CAB customers took time away from work and family to be at the meeting. Sharing CAB insights will validate the value they gained from serving as a customer advisory board member to the supplier company hosting the CAB.

Executive Pro Tip: Don't forget to ask your company executive sponsor to promote the CAB at the next all-hands.

It is extremely important to share with employees what customers think. There are also a lot of teams that support the CAB, so make sure they get recognition and kudos. I wish I had done more in my early career to acknowledge everyone who contributed to the CAB.

Don't Forget to Circle Back to Sales and Customer Success

Two weeks after the executive summary is distributed, the company executive sponsor or the CAB lead should set up a meeting to review the highlights of the CAB with sales and customer success (CS). I'd start with the executive summary, and then dive into the CAB customers by each account.

I believe it's vital, now more than ever, to give the sales and CS people who nominated the customers for the board access to the details of the meeting. After a CAB, sales and CS people will quickly follow up with their customers partly to be attentive, and partly because they were not invited to this intimate board gathering and they are curious what the CAB was like for their customers. With smartphones, communication is done in nanoseconds; customers may even be texting or emailing their sales or customer success managers during the CAB or right after the CAB is over. It's more work, but going the extra mile and attending to details is part of being world class. Providing sales and CS with CAB customers' likes and concerns will help them strategically manage their customer accounts. Overall, it's a great way for your executives to ask for the CS team to help set up any future one-on-ones with a CAB customer. For example, a CS will know an account's typical weekly calendar. The CS and CAB customer may already have a standing meeting every two weeks on a Tuesday at 1:00 p.m.

Going Forward: The Minimal Approach to CAB Sponsor Outreach

You've all run out of steam and need to get back to your daily roles in your company. I understand. At a minimum, after a CAB meeting ask executives to make at least one call or have a video conference with their assigned customer. Suggest the executives ask the following three questions during their meeting.

1. Overall, what did you think of the CAB?

2. What did you like and dislike about the CAB?

3. How can we make the CAB experience better for you?

These are simple post-CAB meeting questions that make it easier for customers to candidly share what they liked and didn't like. The questions also make it easier for you to analyze the feedback since they are the same for all the customers. And, of course, the executive and the customer should be encouraged to ask their own questions.

Make sure if you decide to take this minimal outreach approach that you close out any lingering questions and resolve outstanding issues.

I am not a huge fan of minimal post-CAB member outreach and recommend a formal sponsorship program (see page 142), but there are additional steps you can take to elevate the quality of your company's communications with customers, improve outcomes, and elevate your CAB program to the next level.

Elevating How You Communicate with Your Customers

Taking CABs to the next level didn't really happen in my career until I had eight CAB programs under my belt. This was partly due to my role and my fear of displeasing executives. My role as the CAB lead was just one of my responsibilities as a customer reference or customer advocate. My daily responsibilities were sourcing and managing customer interviews for sales and marketing references. Whenever anyone in the company wanted the use of a customer's logo, quote, or customer to speak either privately or publicly about their deployment, they came through me or my team. Time and needs don't stop because you're running a CAB.

It did bug me that I wasn't able to do more for the customers who sat on the board or get more benefit out of the CAB for company executives. On a seriously challenging road bike ride up Montebello Road in Cupertino, California, I was huffing and puffing for my life when I realized it wasn't my other responsibilities that were holding back the CAB program; it was my fear. I'm naturally a pleaser, so post-CAB meeting I didn't want to wrangle the executives who didn't contact their appointed CAB customer every quarter.

In my head, I listed the benefits to customers and executive of having quarterly calls: They would gain a kinship by tackling similar challenges and sharing insights on how to grow their business and keep their operation expenses low, and they would gain more awareness for their business and teams. The list flowed naturally. I realized that the CAB was a trust experience for both the customer and vendor leaders. Although they came from different worlds with different perspectives, they could bond over their mutual interest in the product or service and technology.

From talking to executives, I realized that part of the problem was some executives lacked experience with this type of customer follow-up and needed training and support to build a rapport with their customer and a good working relationship. Most executives I spoke to wanted to connect with customers, but they needed a guide or a cheat sheet on how to engage with their assigned customer board member.

Often, the reason people don't follow through isn't because they forget. It's because they don't want to deliver bad news.

Delivering Bad News, or "No, We Can't ..."

Communicating difficult information to a CAB sponsor, such as a product/service request that won't be built, can be challenging for some company leaders who are "pleasers," inexperienced, and/ or very cautious about what to say. Instead of communicating openly and honestly, they may try to avoid the issue by ignoring the CAB sponsor. When this happens, it can take a team effort to get communication back on track.

Executive Pro Tip: Always be honest.

The best way to convey difficult news or answer a tough question is to be honest. Customers will respect you even more.

The following are examples of customer messages I received as the CAB lead and how I facilitated a response.

Example 1: "I asked your COO to get back to me about my annual renewal and am hoping to get a discount, but I haven't heard back. I'm about to renew in two weeks. What's going on?"

Internal resolution: First check with the COO to learn whether they've asked the sales leader who attended the CAB to work with the account executive for a discount. If not, the CAB lead should follow up with an email to the sales leader and copy the COO. Clearly ask the sales leader to determine who will follow up and when they follow up with the customer.

Sales leader's response in an internal email: Yes, I sat next to the CAB customer during breakfast. I know her. I'll work directly with their account executive. We will follow up by the end of the day. CC: COO.

Action from CAB lead: Email the CAB customer. Acknowledge we dropped the ball, and that the sales leader will be responding with the account executive by the end of day. CC: COO, sales leader, account executive, and CSM.

Example 2: "I don't know what's taking so long. I thought I would hear by now from the chief product officer (CPO) if they can add the feature, especially since it would surely win more customers for our customers."

Internal resolution: First check with the CPO to see if they can personally reach out or offer to set up a meeting with the CAB customer.

CPO's response in an internal email: Yes, I dropped the ball. We aren't going to get to this feature request because we're focused on new product features. I need to talk to custom engineering to determine whether they can possibly build this feature for our CAB member. Please help me follow up and schedule a meeting but give me forty-eight hours to see if I can get custom engineering to scope the work.

Action from CAB lead: Email the CAB customer. Acknowledge we dropped the ball and that the CPO is in the loop. They apologized and asked me to set up a meeting in three days to connect on the feature request.

Most CAB customers just want a response. The CAB customer has to decide on priorities for their business. Board customers want to be acknowledged, listened to, and respected by your leaders, and company executives can assure them they are being heard by following up. Not following up and not following through can have a negative impact on the entire CAB program and your company's brand. As a CAB lead, I encourage you to provide whatever support your executives need to make follow-up frictionless and to be ready to smooth any wrinkles that emerge when a customer request falls through the cracks. A formal CAB Sponsorship Program (page 142) helps.

Additionally, if an executive can't follow up for any reason, make sure you have one to three executives who can fill in. Choose executives who have a high emotional IQ. They are often the chief customer officer, vice president of support, or vice president of customer success.

If you're concerned that there will be a lot of requests or follow-up that could be sensitive, it's best to ask the company executive sponsor to nominate an internal VP or a higher leader to have these ongoing difficult conversations. There are leaders who are much better at delivering bad news. Have those leaders identified before the CAB meeting and offer them a seat on the CAB, so they can support your post-CAB follow-up.

Dealing with Poor CAB Sponsor Follow-Through

No matter what you do as the CAB lead to encourage communication between executives and customers, you'll likely still get customer complaints about poor executive follow-up. It's one of the most common complaints I received from customer advisory board members. Whether the CAB was for a start-up or a mature company, I would get an email or text from a customer telling me how awesome the CAB was, how they got along so well with the C-suite, how they were so surprised by all the new features, and thank me for my hard work. But then they would say what's really on their mind: an executive promised to follow up, but no one had.

I dealt with these messages by taking the feedback seriously. I would tell the customer I'd look into it and have a response within twelve hours. I would be honest and tell them my response may not solve the issue, but I would get back to them with an update. As the CAB lead, I would typically drop what I was working on to deal with the customer's issue. Why? I had worked very hard at the CAB event to create a positive experience and build trust between executives and board members, and I wanted to make sure the customer feels heard and respected. And these "ball drops" could have a ripple effect. A customer could bad-mouth us to a peer board member.

When a customer reaches out with an issue, such as poor follow-through, remain focused on doing what's right for the customer advisory board member and be sure to elevate your communication style to maintain a good relationship.

World-Class Post-CAB Meeting Practice: A Formal CAB Sponsorship Program

Having a formalized program provides structure for executive follow-up and can change the way your customers view your products or services. CAB members may prioritize you over other vendors because of the relationship that has developed after the CAB meeting. The connections made between executives and customers can lead to partnership, openness, support, and, ultimately, lifelong friendships.

A formal CAB sponsorship program organizes and tracks the quarterly follow-up meetings between a CAB sponsor and a board customer. These meetings are when executives reach out to ask our customer advisers to reconnect, vet ideas, and talk about what's new.

In my experience, a formal program will help reciprocity develop between customers and executives. Executives will have access to valuable market insights and board customers will have access to executives if they need to escalate issues. (When they do, CAB customers should get the VIP treatment.)

If you think establishing a formal program seems like too much work, I encourage you to revisit your perception of the CAB's value. Your customers are the reason for your company's success, and they should be treated with appreciation and respect. A world-class CAB event is intended to build meaningful connections, and you want to be careful that the post-CAB experience doesn't diminish those connections and reduce your CAB meeting to a one-off engagement with executives. The worst-case scenario when that happens is executives are perceived as disingenuous when they call a CAB customer for help, advice, or to speak at industry conferences down the road. Your company put a lot of resources into the CAB; the post-CAB meeting period is the time to maximize its benefits, and a formal program is one of the best ways to do so.

Naveed, the Ivy League university CIO whose thoughts on CABs appeared in chapter 1, was one of my first enterprise customers who advised on developing professional services and customer success teams. He had this to say about post-CAB quarterly meetings:

I've always enjoyed my quarterly calls with the COO. We developed not only a business relationship, but a friendship as well. We would run ideas by each other. Before their yearly user conference, I and a few other board members were asked to listen to the COO keynote. We've seen him speak before at the CAB, so we felt very comfortable providing two rounds of feedback. And it was also fun just getting a few of the board members together to catch up.

Asking your executives to participate in a formal sponsorship program for the rest of the year can be challenging. To make the argument for one, here are three real outcomes from having executives engage with CAB customers every quarter.

- A CAB sponsor, a CTO, and the CAB customer, also a CTO, discussed what kind of orchestration and workflows they would want so they could move away from the leading infrastructure-as-a-service (IaaS). By learning and building out the new automations, they became top competitors against the leading IaaS.

- After a regional EMEA CAB, the largest mass-media CAB customer became advocates in the truest sense. They offered the UK's largest supermarket company an on-site visit to understand their technical and business decisions for moving to a unified-communication-as-a-service offering.

- A unified-communications-as-a-service (UCaaS) company grew 30 percent year over year with a CAB. The post-CAB customer advocacy calls helped develop customer C-suite-level relationships. Previously, the UCaaS company only had access to directors.

Two Ways to Run a Formal Program

There are two ways to run a post-CAB meeting program to deepen your relationship with customers:

1. **Have the CAB lead manage all the details and prompt executives to set up their next one-on-one CAB quarterly meetings.** The upside to having the CAB lead manage the program is it's easier to track the follow-up calls and make sure the details of the calls are logged into the CAB Customer Dashboard/Profiles spreadsheet in a timely fashion (see page 146 for an example of an updated spreadsheet). It takes the responsibility of uploading information into the spreadsheet off the executives' plates. All they have to do is forward the conversation details to the CAB lead to enter. The downside

is the full responsibility of post-CAB meeting follow-up is on the CAB lead. Having one person doing everything doesn't scale with more than ten customers. They will also have to make sure to update the entire CAB account team after each follow-up: CAB executive sponsor, sales manager, and customer success manager, and anyone else who would likely connect with the customer directly, such as a professional services manager.

2. **Have the CAB lead partner with each CSM whose customer sits on the board to help facilitate the CAB quarterly meetings for the CAB sponsor.** Over time, these meetings could become CSM and executive in-person visits. The visit can turn into a midyear executive briefing for the customer and a chance for the executive and CSM to meet other customers' leaders. This supports the CSM goal of upselling and/or introducing new functionalities of features or services. Although you could have a sales lead shoulder these post-CAB meeting responsibilities, arranging for a CSM to coordinate will resonate well with the customer because follow-ups will become less salesy and more focused on the success of the customer. CSMs will also have the challenge of keeping all internal stakeholders up to date with the CAB customer meetings.

Post-CAB Customer Dashboard/Profiles

On the next page, there is an example of how to update the CAB Customer Dashboard/Profiles spreadsheet with follow up and notes.

Name	Ron Peni
Title	CIO
Email	rp@xp.com
Company/ Industry	XP/ Consulting
Product in use	1, 2, 3, 4
Professional Services	Yes, for custom onboarding
Current sales opportunities	Stage 4: 3 more products of 1
Support tickets?	Yes, tier 1 (days open 2), closed
Rep/CSM/ PS	Kim P./ Mike M./Gary S.
Global?	Brazil and Japan
Partner	IBM
Post: Questions and concerns	Roadmap: UX question
Post: Ex. Sponsor follow-up when?	6/7/24 inviting head of UX
Post 1st exec mtg: One-on-one summary	UX head took feedback and asked if CAB customers would like to see the next early designs to contribute to the final design decisions.
Post 1st exec mtg, status, next steps	8/20/24 next meeting and inviting head of UX and head of Design

CAB Sponsor Outreach and the Timing of the Meeting

The CAB outreach has to be strategic. I have found that having these meetings in the middle of a quarter works best. If you try to talk to your customers at the end of the quarter, they will be too busy with their own corporate initiatives. It's likely your executives will also be very focused on their own business objectives. Having the meeting mid-quarter will provide your executive and customer more time to connect and have a more thoughtful conversation than a quick check-in. Regardless of what cadence or schedule you have with your CAB customers, make sure CAB sponsors stick to it.

If there's an emergency before a quarterly meeting, don't let the customer down. Ask another CAB sponsor to attend the meeting. It's important to tell the customer board member of the emergency, but it's best not to reschedule, unless the customer requests it. The quarterly meetings between your executive vendor sponsor and customer board member will lead to an everlasting relationship with your customer, but to get to this point, being consistent is key.

How to Prepare Your Executives for their CAB Quarterly Meetings

The very first meeting between the executive and the CAB member should be a one-on-one virtual meeting for two important reasons: to build trust and to get to know each other. Often, customers want to convey feedback only to the executive. If the customer and CAB sponsor know each other well, meaning they have bonded well during the CAB meeting, the executive can ask the CAB customer if it makes sense to have other people from their teams join in the conversation. For example, if the customer has questions about support, the CAB customer may want to have their super administrator of the CAB product at the meeting, and the CAB sponsor may want to invite an internal support expert to find solutions and actions. But let the customer lead; they may simply want to have a one-on-one with their sponsor.

Before the quarterly follow-up meeting, the CAB lead or CSM should provide the CAB sponsor with an updated CAB Customer Dashboard/Profiles with the most recent customer account data. Every executive who calls their CAB customer will need this customer data. Add the new fields into the existing post-CAB Customer Dashboard/Profile spreadsheet. These customer account fields include information on how the account is doing, to help direct their conversation. A few additional fields should be added.

Post-CAB Customer Dashboard/Profiles with Additional Account Information (Prep for Future Quarterly Follow-Up Calls)

Any flags on the account?	Level of support	Date of last support case?	Status of support	Last sales date	Last sales type	Is there an active sales opportunity?	Who last spoke to the customer board member?
Yes, PS Account	Platinum	05/06/24	Pending customer response	03/06/23	PS	No	Maria, VP of PS

Additionally, two more internal actions need to happen to prep your CAB sponsor for their meeting with the CAB customer.

- Provide the executive with this background information and talking points on one page.

- Check with the relevant salesperson and their customer success person for any recent issues or developments.

Executive Pro Tip: Keep the Post-CAB Customer Dashboard/ Profiles spreadsheet confidential.

Limit access to the spreadsheet to better protect sensitive information, password protect it and change it every quarter. Another option is for the CAB lead to pull only the appointed customer's information for each CAB sponsor.

That said, I don't share the CAB Customer Dashboard/Profiles spreadsheet often, because there's too much data and it will be difficult for an executive to review. Instead, I provide a new tab within the spreadsheet. I have one master tab that has all the content from before the CAB to the post-CAB event. I create a new tab in the spreadsheet showing only the newest CAB activities to help the executive focus on the current details.

After all the CAB sponsors have spoken to their customers each quarter, I suggest creating one slide for the CEO and company executive sponsor to update them.

How to Collect Notes on CAB Conversations

Tracking CAB customer follow-ups can be very difficult. There may be some one-on-one conversations that the CAB lead or CSM isn't privy to, but it's still important for the post-CAB meeting program lead to do their best to diligently track each meeting executives have with the customer board member and to collect the feedback. The best way to track calls is to work with the executive assistant or chief of staff and have them set up the quarterly customer video conference meetings with the customer board member. Many video conference systems now have transcription functionality, which makes it easier to log the interactions between the board member and CAB sponsor.

If there's no support staff, it's easiest to use a company texting app, like Google or Slack, to ask executives to share feedback. As the CAB lead, you'll have to create and update the CAB Customer Dashboard/Profiles spreadsheet with information (see page 146 for an example) or add it into custom CRM fields.

I'm a big advocate of partnering with the CSM of a CAB customer. If they can manage future executive conversations, they can ensure the details of conversations will be logged in a system (such as a CRM or a CSM and/or Customer Advocate software). I also believe having the CSM drive the CAB sponsorship calls with the CAB member will help with CSM upselling goals.

It will always be frustrating to collect information from post-CAB executive conversations with customers. If you know a call happened, try to capture at least the date, time, and high-level topics discussed.

Creating an Escalation Process for Your CAB Customers

The challenge in running the CAB sponsorship program is building a support escalation route for a CAB member's request.

Josh is a lead of product strategy for one of the most successful software-as-a-service (SaaS) companies of all time. He's responsible for a portfolio of products that generates over $6 billion in annual subscription revenue across several business units and dozens of products. He led, spoke at, and attended more than a hundred CABs. He hit the nail on the head when it comes to the necessity of having a clear escalation process when he shared his post-CAB meeting experiences:

> *Executive account sponsorship programs are difficult to run after a CAB. Often the executive is put in a position where they have no control. For example, the CIO of our company might be the CAB sponsor for a CAB member. If that CAB member then has a product issue that requires an escalation, our CIO doesn't have the knowledge or authority to help other than trying to find the right people inside our organization. My suggestion for someone who is running the CAB is to make sure there is a process or escalation path for CAB requests and that CAB sponsors have explicit authority to act on behalf of customers. Make it clear to CAB sponsors how to support their CAB customers.*

Another reason to partner with the CSM is they already have an internal process for escalations. The CSM can add a higher priority to the request because it's from a CAB customer.

If you don't have a CAB escalation process, I suggest you don't recreate the wheel. Go to the head of customer success and ask if you can help them adapt the existing escalation process already in place to better serve CAB customers. For example, ask for the support leader to create a report on any net-new support tickets for each CAB customer and have the report automatically sent to the relevant CAB sponsor. All the stakeholders—the account team, customer success manager, professional services team, and CAB lead—should be copied.

Keeping CAB Sponsors Accountable

To keep CAB sponsors accountable, create a CAB quarterly internal report including a one-page update on each CAB account. I like creating this report mid-quarter, a week before the call. If you pull the data too early, it won't be current. I would even double-check the customer account to make sure the data is current the morning of the executive sponsorship call. The spreadsheet is supposed to make it easy for the executive to review their assigned CAB customer. The internal report can help nudge executives who haven't set up their meetings with their CAB customers yet. Note, creating this report can be labor intensive, so you may not want to be subtle. An obvious nudge is to highlight in light red the name of CAB sponsors who are behind on their meetings.

Pro Tip: It's really hard to chase executives down. It's not personal.

They're focused on their part of the business. Set up gentle reminders on their calendars to review the current CAB quarterly internal report one week before the quarterly meetings. Share the report with the executive assistants. With the support of their executive assistants, the quarterly meetings will go off without a hitch.

Replacing a CAB Sponsor

If an executive leaves or isn't following up, the CAB lead or CSM should consult with the company executive sponsor to choose another executive who was at the CAB meeting to take over the sponsorship. If an executive sponsor switch is made, have the new CAB sponsor reach out to the customer, share on the phone why they are the new sponsor, and explain that the previous CAB sponsor left the company or was too busy. The company executive sponsor should also reach out to the customer and explain why they selected the executive to be their new sponsor—for example, they share the same background, or the customer is mostly concerned with a part of the sponsor's line of business. The CAB lead can write the email for the company executive sponsor to send out before they have a call with the new sponsor.

Getting CAB Customer Feedback

It's standard practice to send out a post-event survey. Over the years, however, I've found the data to have inflated scores. This is often because customers want to keep their CAB seat.

While five-star ratings for the CAB program certainly raises awareness and may help secure the future CAB budget, I decided to stop asking CAB customers to fill out surveys. Instead, I want candid feedback, and that's best done one-on-one over the phone or via video conference. The CAB lead should start the conversation with these three questions:

1. Overall, what did you think of the CAB?

2. What did you like and dislike about the CAB?

3. How can we make the CAB experience better for you?

These three questions will open up your CAB members. Listen, take notes, and learn.

How to Manage CAB Alumni

A CAB alumnus is a customer who attended a past CAB meeting but is no longer in your CAB program. A CAB alumni program can be a wonderful benefit for both the vendor and the customer.

There's no right or wrong way to structure a CAB alumni program. At a minimum, you can have a biannual one-to-two-hour update over a webinar to give these CAB alumni VIP information. For instance, you can share, before the news is public, that the company is bringing in a new VP of Product who will be in charge of building out your new artificial intelligence (AI) features.

Another alumni perk is to offer annual or biannual CAB connection calls, where the CAB lead would reach out to each customer to ask if they would like to have a one-on-one with a CAB sponsor.

You may want to offer an executive hotline that the CAB lead or a CSM will manage as your executive concierge inside the company. These are great perks to grow your customer advocates and keep engaged with your CAB customers.

The frequency of contact is up to the CAB lead and CAB sponsor. For example, if you're looking to grow your business in another industry, you may want to keep constant contact with your alumni from that industry.

Double-check with your CMO and CRO on their goals. If they want to target certain decision-makers for field events and/or sponsor conferences, you'll likely want to invest more time in building out your alumni program. You may want to plan what kind of customer presentations you'd likely need first and then go back into your CAB profiles to see if there's a good fit among your CAB customers to attend these events and speak at them.

Asking a CAB Customer to Speak at a Conference or Field Event

After the CAB meeting, you'll want your customers to act as advocates for the company and take sales reference calls or speak with analysts. CMOs and CROs will request CAB customers speak at future conferences or field events. During the CAB meeting, it's a good idea to jot down who you think would be great at sharing their story in this way. When you know of a speaking opportunity, ask the CAB customer right away. Don't assume just because they're on the board they will make your request a priority.

When asking your CAB customer to speak at an event, please don't pitch the speaking opportunity as a testimonial. Build a pitch that promotes the customer as a thought leader and their talk as a way to promote themselves, their company, and their team. Determine which other panels, conference activities, or press events you'd want your customer to attend and ask them if they'd be willing to participate in those as well. Always think about your customer's experience at these events and never assume they will be available. You never want the customer to feel you are taking advantage of them.

Also, be sure to ask the customer to get approval from their management and legal teams to speak publicly. There is a higher likelihood the customer will receive approval because they sit on the board, but it's always best to double-check with your customer and their legal team.

Above all, treat your customers like VIP keynote speakers. For example, let's say you want to invite a dynamic customer to speak at a local conference. Your customer lives eighty miles away but is willing to drive to the event. Your customer will be going out of their way to prepare to speak publicly, network, be an on-the-spot customer reference, and be away from their family, so make traveling easy for them. Order a ride-sharing service to pick them up and drop them home, so they don't have to worry about driving or parking. Offer to host them overnight at the same hotel as your team. The next morning, invite them to breakfast either with the entire team or just one-on-one with an executive. Learn what they thought of the event and who they met.

> **Pro Tip:** Here's how to ask your dynamic CAB speaker to speak at more events!
>
> When you have an amazing CAB speaker, you always want to ask them to speak at other locations. My secret to getting customers to say yes is to be honest with them and tell them they are top speakers. To entice them, offer them speaking opportunities in cities that are notoriously fun. For example, I knew a customer who loved baseball, so I flew them from Seattle to Chicago for a field event and then got them tickets to a Chicago Cubs game. You can also suggest a city where the speaker has a satellite office, so they can drop into their own office to meet their colleagues.

CAB Sponsorship Programs Are Worth the Work

You may be reading this and thinking, "CABs are a lot of work. Are they really worth it?" Consider this analogy: When a couple has a wedding, it's a big to-do. Typically, tens of thousands of dollars are spent for less than ten hours of celebration. Once the wedding is over, the couple must now sustain their marriage. Marriages that last have two key components: communication and a willingness to work at it.

Investing in a CAB is similar to investing in a wedding. You spend money and time on a special day to engage and build trust with your customer advisory board. Once the meeting is over, your company must continue to invest to sustain the relationship.

With the information in this chapter, I hope you can form a CAB sponsorship program for you and your executives to help you not just keep in touch with your customers but to develop more trust and lifelong friendships with them. Life is short, and we spend a lot of time at work. Let's make it meaningful. Let's create more human connections with our customers.

Chapter 6 covered the following:

- What you should do directly after a CAB.

- The importance of following up with customers after a CAB, and how to prepare and conduct an executive summary meeting.

- How to handle situations where executives aren't communicating with their customers, and how to help them maintain positive customer relationships.

- How to run a formal CAB sponsorship program that will keep new and seasoned CAB customers connected with your company.

In the next chapter, you'll learn how to host an effective virtual CAB that executives, customers, and speakers can join from anywhere.

7
HOSTING A WORLD-CLASS VIRTUAL CAB

Before the COVID-19 global pandemic, it was practically unheard of to have a virtual CAB meeting. Company executives wanted to connect in person with their customers. Even small start-ups had physical CAB events.

In post-pandemic times, small, midsize, and enterprise B2B companies and customers still crave face-to-face connection. However, it's still challenging to hold a two-day CAB off-site. Budget and scheduling constraints are the main hurdles. Overall, business travel has been reduced, and it will take a long time for people to travel like they did before the pandemic. People are less inclined to travel for business due to fewer direct flights and the stress of dealing with airlines, airports, and weather delays. Instead of meeting face-to-face, it's more convenient for CAB members to meet from the comfort of their own home or office. As a result, customers and companies have embraced virtual CAB events. The biggest reason to go virtual is to cut costs. Companies can have a virtual CAB meeting for a fraction of what it costs to have a physical one.

Virtual CAB meetings do offer an opportunity to make connections, but I'm still a big believer in in-person CAB experiences. The major downside to holding a virtual CAB event is that the experience is through a laptop or stand-alone monitor. In the virtual world, it's hard to keep people engaged, and there's no downtime with the board members. The downtime—planned as well as impromptu, such as when waiting for an elevator—provides opportunities for attendees to connect during breaks and meals. During a real-time, in-person experience, people become close, build rapport, and gain a deeper connection. To be fair, small group breakaway meetings can be organized in the virtual world to make networking easier, but it's simply not as easy to make meaningful connections through a screen.

That means that a CAB lead hosting a virtual CAB needs to focus on methodically building networking opportunities in the preplanning stage of the virtual CAB. To have an engaging virtual CAB for the customer and the executives it's so important to have more video conference meetings. For example, walk the customer through the agenda before the CAB starts and ask them what they will ask and/or what they could please consider asking. Most important, ask both your customers and executives to sincerely ask questions and share ideas. The goal of this virtual CAB is to make sure they get value from being on the board.

These details may sound like "oh, yeah, normal," but I encourage you not to take adequate prep or active participation for granted or as a given. We have become so used to hopping on video conference calls that we don't spend enough time maximizing the time we have with one another on them. Expect that the virtual CAB can take up to six months to plan.

In this chapter, I'll share best practices for a virtual CAB and my secret sauce for building connections virtually. Note that many of the best practices for hosting a world-class virtual event overlap with hosting an in-person event. If you skipped chapters 3 and 4, I encourage you to go back to them now as they provide an essential foundation for this chapter. But before you jump back to chapters 3 and 4, let me share some big must-haves for building your virtual CAB.

- Be respectful of the customers and company executives' time. That means, put a lot of effort in preparation, presenters, the balance of content, and the length of the CAB. Below are things to make a priority when it comes to planning your virtual CAB.

- Preparation: Prep both the customers and executives

  - Think about how to get your customers and executives to engage. That starts with setting up a pre-meeting, walking them through the agenda, and telling them where we need their help to engage. Ask them where they will likely ask questions or provide feedback. If they are quiet, ask them to pick areas of the agenda to be ready to speak up.

- Virtual CAB Presenters: It's not always the smartest person in the room

  - There's a lot of cachet for the customers on the board to build a relationship with company executives. However, some of the executives aren't expressive or don't have the energy to keep people engaged. It takes a special person in the company. Therefore, recruit your two to three most engaging internal speakers to co-present. For example, if your new product owner is dry, have them partner with a high-energy internal speaker. Then let the product owner engage with customers.

- Balance of content: It's actually harder to retain online content than in person

  - The web conference platform is seen as an "easy" button/ solution to run a CAB. Most people who have been working through the pandemic are used to two ways of really using a web conference: There's the one-on-one, where you are looking directly at them and engaging—you'll learn, engage, yes! Then there are the updates, like a webinar readout of information. We are used to a lot of those; we have probably used a webinar-like meeting in our roles, where we present an update. If you have been the audience, you likely multitasked or lost focus. It's just natural. These settings are now in muscle memory. The virtual CAB should have no more than twelve people on camera, and you have to keep the content of every CAB succinct. The goal is cross-engagement. The company host needs to have content that is focused. There can be no, "Hey, let's show them our entire roadmap for one hour to impress our CAB, and then go back to features that your executive(s) have concerns with." Instead, build your presentation to focus on what exactly you want feedback on from your customers. You'll have to explain this to them. I find by explaining, customers perk up and focus better during the virtual CAB.

- Length of the CAB: Keep it short, under two hours

  o There may be some balking that two hours is too short. Correct, so keep to no more than three important messages or questions you want to discuss with your customer advisers. Factor in that not only are you presenting, but you need time to encourage discussion and back-and-forth between customers and executives. It's important. But less really is more. And you can create a two- or three-part series. That's my secret sauce: creating a virtual CAB series.

  o Let's flip this example. Say I want to have a three-hour CAB. We could start in the midmorning, break for lunch, and resume in the afternoon. A rookie mistake is to pile all the agenda items in one meeting. You'll lose someone's interest. (We've all lost interest.) Once you start to lose engagement, some people will start to multitask, some will watch and listen, and some will zone out. All the work and the time you took to pull your customers and executives away, and they will likely retain only 20 percent of what was presented and discussed. The negative outcome: the board will not feel excited, but more likely will feel that the CAB was long and flat. Customers may not be impressed with your board.

There are plenty of tips in this chapter, along with my secret sauce that will help you build a virtual CAB that will meet your goals. Before we get into them, let's review the pros and cons of a virtual CAB.

Pros and Cons of Virtual CABs

If you're considering hosting a virtual CAB meeting, keep these pros and cons in mind.

- Pros of a virtual CAB meeting

    - Inexpensive and uses web conference technology

    - Easier to schedule, usually lasts three hours instead of two days

    - Convenient—doesn't require travel and the hassles that go with it

    - Popular with CAB members for the same reasons remote work is popular with employees: virtual is more convenient. Customers don't have to travel or be away from family.

- Cons of a virtual CAB meeting

    - Hard to maintain people's attention

- o No shared downtime among CAB members
- o Need to work harder to establish connections
- o Due to limited time it can feel hurried and superficial, only skimming the surface
- o Often only have time to focus on one or two issues
- o Can feel rigid with a tight, fixed agenda and limited discussion time
- o Harder to read facial expressions and body language
- o May need to have several CAB meetings to cover what one physical meeting can
- o Start-and-stop nature makes it harder to build relationships and trust
- o Difficult to draw out the root of the issue
- o Takes longer to solve problems and/or find solutions

Though there is a long list of cons, I want to assure you that if you decide to go the virtual route (or management decides for you!) you've totally got this. You can host a world-class virtual CAB with the tips and strategies in this chapter. If you really want to have a physical CAB, you could share this pros and cons list with your executives and give asking for a physical CAB budget another try.

Virtual CAB Customers
How Many Customers to Invite

Invite six virtual customer board members to the virtual meeting and have only six executives attend. Having only six customers may seem like too few given the amount of work it takes to host a CAB, but think about your leaders. The CAB meeting is for your executives to form long-lasting connections with strategic customers and should be a 1:1 ratio. The sweet spot is six customers.

Six customers on your virtual CAB ensures a great flow of conversation among members during the virtual meeting. Adding any more will make it extremely difficult to facilitate conversation. Fewer than six customers and your executives may not have enough perspectives to get well-rounded or in-depth advice from the board.

The virtual format can also make it difficult to garner enough feedback from a smaller board. Often, not all the CAB members will have a response to a question, or one or two board members may get shy. Some customers may not feel respected for their input or not be asked to engage. Discussions might be dominated by the most verbose customer, simultaneously suppressing and annoying the quieter board members. In the planning stage, it's crucial to choose customers who feel comfortable openly sharing over a virtual event, but even so, with fewer than six board members you risk hosting an unproductive CAB meeting.

If your CAB executive sponsor feels it's important to garner additional customer feedback, consider having another virtual CAB meeting with six other customers, perhaps in a different region of the world or focused on a different customer profile. If you want more discussions, have more frequent CAB alumni meetings.

Virtual CAB Customer Criteria and Nominations

The main criteria for choosing customers for an in-person CAB covered in chapter 3 (page 52) also apply for a virtual CAB. For a virtual CAB, the number one criterion that shouldn't be overlooked is a customer's soft skills. You will want a customer to speak up and articulate their thoughts in a virtual environment. It's harder to read the room when looking into a monitor.

Here's the list of questions you can use to help gauge a customer's soft skills during a virtual interview:

- When I'm speaking to them, do they make eye contact?

- When I'm speaking to them, are they multitasking?

- When I ask them questions about being a part of the CAB, are they responding with enthusiasm and interest? Or are they dull and uninterested?

- Have they asked any questions about the CAB format? (If they have asked questions, take it as a good indication that the customer cares and will likely turn out to be a strong adviser.)

It's important for you to trust your gut. If the nominated CAB customer is eating their lunch or picking their teeth (yes, this happened to me) when meeting online, they will not be a good fit for your board.

If your nominated customers are excited and you feel it in your gut that they would really mesh well with your executives, then go right into walking them through the mission and high-level agenda to secure their spot. Once they agree, ask them to provide an introduction video to be shared ahead of time with everyone attending the virtual meeting (see page 175 for an outline of what the customer should include in the video) and send them an email outlining deadlines. Treat your customer board members as you would internal company executives. Send out meeting invites with deadline reminders for signing the mutual NDA and submitting their video introduction.

Executive Pro Tip: Always enlist a customer veteran who has served on a CAB.

Have at least one customer board member who has served on a CAB. Most CAB customers can aid as facilitators and even help other customers open up during the board meeting.

Customers who were previous CAB members are often the best fit for a virtual CAB. Their experience gives them confidence, they're less nervous and not worried about what other people think of their comments. These customers are comfortable speaking up and often naturally facilitate discussions and/or ask what their peers think. Peers with past CAB experience will encourage other board members to open up and share their experiences.

Set Expectations with Customers Before the CAB Meeting

To create sincere CAB virtual interactions, the CAB lead needs to prepare the customer ahead of time. It's important to bring up the physical limitations of a virtual CAB meeting.

A few business days before the virtual CAB meeting, the CAB lead should arrange calls with customer board members to review the final agenda. This can be one-on-one, or you can host a couple of pre–virtual CAB meeting walkthroughs.

During this meeting, give a short introduction about each customer on the board to show the CAB was formed strategically and not slapped together. Then review the agenda.

CAB Lead Pro Tip: Find commonality between your board members and share that before the CAB meeting.

Before you meet with your CAB member, research and select one to three other customers who have something in common with them. For example, mention that another board member has a master's degree or grew up in the South. This helps with getting customers comfortable.

When reviewing the agenda, you'll need to feel confident in the sessions and be able to go in-depth on what will be shared. If you're uncomfortable, invite a product expert or a VP of product marketing who can do a great job pumping up the board member(s).

CAB Lead Pro Tip: Provide your CAB customer with a preview of the CAB agenda.

The CAB customer may not be familiar with all of your product's features or offerings. Walk them through a preview of the virtual CAB agenda so they have enough time to prepare and ask their team for their insights. This is important because you want to make sure customers come to the virtual CAB to speak, not to sit back and listen.

Have everyone who's on the board prepare by asking them to develop questions based on the agenda session topics. By doing so, the board meeting experience will be positive and much more interactive. The entire board and your leadership will feel satisfied that giving their time and insights during the CAB meeting was time well spent. They will look forward to future CAB virtual events.

A Webinar/Web Conference System Is Worth the Investment

Don't skimp by using a freemium video conference platform. Look at investing in a web conference solution for your virtual CAB meeting.

Here are some features to consider for your web conference solution:

- **Virtual lobby:** If you're the sole CAB person leading the meeting, you'll want a system that has a virtual lobby to welcome everyone.

- **Annotation:** There are tools that let you annotate documents during the meeting, which provides an increased opportunity for interaction.

- **Polling:** During the product or service roadmap, using polling to increase engagement has its upsides and downsides. Polls are great, but they take up time from discussions. Online polls can also cause a snafu if the person who runs the polls doesn't have experience using them. Often a webinar administrator can help. Don't leave it up to the main speaker to also run the webinar controls.

- **Breakout rooms:** Often CAB members will have other ideas or even want to break off into a discussion. If you plan for breakouts, make sure you have two internal CAB roles, one who moderates the breakout sessions and one who takes notes during each of the breakout virtual sessions.

- **Recording and transcription:** It's important to have notetakers, but also use recording and transcription technology to help you get the exact quote. Purchasing a webinar solution with recording and transcription features can save you up to six hours reviewing and cross-analyzing notes. Having a transcription of the CAB can help you get every detail down accurately. And when reaching out to follow up internally or externally, you can cite the CAB transcription as a source of truth. It's money well spent.

Even with technology, gather notes from notetakers who are observing. They should have highlighted key conversations or points made. After reviewing the notes, rewatch the areas of the CAB to review the most poignant aha moments. Watching these moments again will also provide you with concrete actions on how to tweak the next virtual CAB meeting, or how to best follow up with your board members.

Invite Your Customer-Facing Teams: Customer Success and Sales

The biggest upside of running a virtual CAB meeting with a webinar or web conference system is that you'll get to invite other strategic peers to observe off camera (so they don't overwhelm the virtual meeting space), such as customer success and sales. The CAB attendees on camera will be the company executives and customers (in a one-to-one ratio) and guest speakers.

Make sure you let your CAB members know who else will have access to the virtual meeting.

Executive Pro Tip: Investing in a webinar system will allow you to invite your customer-facing teams to attend your virtual CAB meeting.

Hosting a meeting through a webinar product allows other company team members to access the discussion without appearing on camera and making your CAB customers feel uncomfortable because they are outnumbered. You could invite the board's customer success managers to listen, so they can help follow up on customers' questions.

Setting Your Virtual CAB Goals

Creating virtual CAB meeting goals is simpler than for an in-person CAB meeting because you don't have to create an experience for one to two days. But this also means you have to carefully choose the topic you want to discuss during the virtual CAB meeting, which will usually last for two hours. With limited time, prioritize developing trust and an agenda for high engagement over covering multiple topics.

If you're going to ask hairy questions on your virtual CAB meeting, make sure you figure out how much you can pre-share with your board members before the meeting. For example, you may not want to write them a pre-CAB meeting email about going IPO or asking them to help support your next round of funding. If you have NDA topics that you don't feel comfortable sharing over email, the CAB lead should go over the topics over the phone. Make sure the customer signs the CAB mutual NDA before the board meeting.

Map the CAB Goals to the Agenda

In chapter 4, you learned how to map out your goals to your agenda (see page 102). Here's what's in a typical virtual CAB agenda.

Sample of Virtual CAB Agenda

Open and Welcome

Icebreaker

Company Overview

Business Strategy

Discussion

Roadmap

Questions

Thank-You and Close

See page 175 for how to build a two-hour virtual CAB meeting agenda.

It's important to spend time mapping out your goals, especially if this is your first CAB. Use the Mapping CAB Goals to the Agenda spreadsheet template.

Mapping CAB Goals to the Agenda

Topic (est. time)	Speaker	Value for customer	Soft (S) or Hard (H) KPI	Benefits for company	Other

After you take a few passes at filling out this spreadsheet, make sure you show it to your manager for their input and then have the CAB executive sponsor review it. Before distributing it to the executives attending the CAB meeting, make sure it is free of errors and easy to read. Creating a presentation slide of the spreadsheet will impress your leader. Mapping CAB goals to the agenda helps executives think about how best to engage with the customers and build trust with them.

How to Get Higher Engagement During a Virtual CAB Meeting

Everyone who is part of a virtual CAB meeting needs to put a little more effort into engaging and interacting with each other to build connections. A virtual CAB meeting is not a show up and listen event like a webinar (an informational meeting). Respectfully remind everyone connected to the virtual CAB meeting about the need to be more intentional.

A world-class virtual CAB meeting requires additional pre-work, pre-meetings, and pre-communications with internal speakers and customer advisers. Why? The executives and the customers need to feel comfortable expressing themselves during the board meeting over a video conference system and confident that their contribution is important. To make that happen, you'll need to work on building engagement with the customer advisers and remind company executives to be engaging before the virtual CABs.

Overcommunicate

If you're leading the CAB, make sure to overcommunicate. Make it very clear to customers the CAB meeting is not just another online meeting and remind them of what's expected of them. You must communicate the importance of the CAB meeting and their role. Use the Virtual CAB Communication Calendar (see page 172) to plan your outreach to customers and internal speakers.

This calendar helps you plan two months out. Personally, I like at least six months to plan a CAB meeting. However, I know we often don't have that luxury. Note, the company internal speaker and executive sponsor, in addition to the CAB lead, should be communicating with members of the customer board two months before the virtual meeting. By overcommunicating, your executives and customers will be more excited and interested in the virtual CAB meeting and it will be easier to meet your CAB goals.

Virtual CAB Communication Calendar

Virtual CAB Communication Calendar	CAB Lead	Company Internal Speaker	Company Executive Sponsor
2 months before the CAB meeting	Set up calls, review the agenda, ask questions; what questions do they have for the board or the company? Have them sign the mutual NDA and film an introduction video.	Acknowledge they are speaking and be prepared. They must agree to two dry runs and 3 business days for an executive to view their final presentation. Film a welcome/introduction email, express interest and excitement. Thank the customers for joining this CAB.	Acknowledge they are attending and will be following up with customer board members after the meeting. Film a welcome/ introduction email, express interest and excitement. Thank the customers for joining this CAB.
6 weeks before the CAB meeting	Send out a video web page with a password to meet the company executives, speakers, and other CAB advisers. Remind customers to fill out mutual NDA.	Turn in the outline of their presentation, to be reviewed by the executive sponsor of the CAB.	Provide feedback and sign off on moving forward with the speaker's presentation.
4 weeks before the CAB meeting	Promote final agenda, share any new public news. Introduce to the customers their future customer executive sponsors, who will be following up after the virtual CAB.	Create the first draft of their presentation, submit any design requests to the creative team to start working on their presentation.	CAB Advisory Dashboard will be shared across the executive team and assigned customer advisers. Remind executives a week before that all support and sales data will be updated in the dashboard prior to the CAB.
3 weeks before the CAB meeting	Final reminder of mutual NDA and/or film video introduction.		

2 weeks before the CAB meeting		Be ready for the first dry run; this is to focus on handoff, housekeeping details, and feeling comfortable with the web conference platform.	Attend the first dry run and evaluate the content.
1 week before the CAB meeting		Second dry run, real run-through to ensure everyone stays within their session time allotment. Include a few outside people: head of CSM, Support, and Sales. Have them provide feedback.	Attend the 2nd dry run.
3 business days before the CAB meeting	Email customer: agenda, supply any pre-questions to their executive sponsor. Ask them to make sure if they haven't done so, get to know the board, go to the video site.	Speakers hand in their presentations to designer for final edits. Presentation then gets reviewed by CAB lead and then passed on to the executive sponsor for a final review.	Final review of speaker's presentations. If concerned with intellectual property (IP), ask the company attorney to review slides.
24 hours before meeting	Check in with the speaker. Forward final deck to web conference admin to upload, set up system. Test out the URL and password to get into the meeting.		

Share Introduction Videos from the CAB Sponsor, Company Executives, and Customer Board Members

Just as you will have asked the customer board members to provide a pre-meeting introduction video, ask your CAB sponsor and other leaders who plan to present to submit videos too. Written bios are standard, but welcome videos are important because you're trying to build human connections before the board meeting. Please encourage everyone to share a little about their personal background, maybe where they grew up or went to college.

To record and share introduction videos, I like to use a third-party video platform that includes prompts for the speaker to record their own video with their own private link. Spending a little money on a video platform allows you to brand the site, and it's intuitive to record. Plus, these third-party video platforms allow you to share all the introduction videos on the same platform.

If you have a tight budget and are unable to use a third-party platform, use your video conference system to create videos of company executives and ask customers to film a video using their own video conference system, and then have them send you their file. Once you collect all the video files, you can create an unlisted web page that's password protected for the customers and company executive CAB members to watch everyone's introduction videos.

Introduction Video Outline Video for the CAB Sponsor or CEO

- Welcome and thank you for joining our CAB

- Share the CAB mission statement

- What we plan to accomplish (overview of goals)

- Review the CAB cadence or series of meetings

- Offer to have a call with the board advisers before the meeting

- Introduce other CAB executives

    o Mention that they will be the sponsors for any post-CAB communications

- Close with a high-level review of the CAB agenda

Introduction Video Outline for the CAB company executives

- Welcome and thank you for joining our CAB
- Introduce yourself and your role at the company
- What you are interested in learning from the CAB members
- Be positive, and let the customers know how excited you are to have them join your CAB

Introduction Video Outline for the CAB Customer

- First and last name, title, company, and location
  - Have them explain what their company does (produce/offer)
  - Your responsibilities at the company
- IT career background: Could be high-level description or a discussion of their last big project (optional)
- What project(s) they're working on and how long they've been a customer
- What they are curious about or looking forward to as part of the CAB

A Two-Hour Virtual CAB Meeting Agenda

In my experience, two hours is the optimal length of a virtual CAB meeting. It's just long enough to show the company values, and it respects the customer's feedback. It's a sufficient amount of time to start building trust between your customers and your executives.

The following example of a virtual CAB meeting agenda is in Pacific Time (PT). This time is the best for your potential customer board members from different parts of the world to join your virtual

CAB. Try starting at 8:00 a.m. PT. In practice, that means being prepared to open the meeting at 7:45 a.m. If you're looking to have some one-on-one time with a specific member, remember to use a different meeting link.

7:45 a.m. PT: Setup

Start the webinar at 7:45 a.m. PT for the speakers. Give them about five minutes to get their slides uploaded and test any audio and visual functions. Have your webinar or virtual events person in your company manage the production of the live webinar and be present throughout the board meeting.

7:55 a.m. PT: Open the Virtual Conference Room for New Arrivals

Offer a five-minute window for your customer board members to log in and settle. It will make starting at 8:00 a.m. less stressful.

Opening early also gives people time to reset and get their minds ready for the CAB meeting and have a little chitchat.

Note that some people may arrive late from back-to-back meetings. Decide beforehand who you need to wait for before starting on the substance of the meeting and who can be drawn gracefully into the meeting with minimum disruption when they arrive—and how you will ease them in.

8:00–8:10 a.m. PT: Welcome and Housekeeping

The CEO or the company executive sponsor who's supporting your CAB is best to welcome everyone and review the agenda. Mention any housekeeping news or changes. For example, your CTO is running late and will be joining first by phone and later online.

8:10–8:30 a.m. PT: Icebreaker

Icebreakers increase engagement among board members. The company executive sponsor should take the lead and propose a fun question to the group, such as "what is your favorite music experience?" They should encourage everyone to share, go around the virtual space.

8:30–8:50 a.m. PT: Company Update

Ask an executive, typically the CEO or a founder, to share a candid update on the business. Include where the company is going, what they're seeing in the market, and why the board is here to advise.

8:50–9:30 a.m. PT: Discussion Priority Topic 1

An executive will use this time to review a strategy or discuss how to find solutions to fix known issues with the company. Examples of issues could be poor support or lack of training videos for adoptions.

9:30–9:45 a.m. PT: Discuss a New Feature, New Ideas, or a Demo

An entire product or service roadmap can often take three to four hours of discussion to review. Given the length of the virtual meeting, focus on one or two key features curated to your customer advisers, or do a demo. If you want to go outside the bounds of this topic you can mention that after the curated discussion. That will help you decide if it should be a part of your next CAB.

9:45–10:00 a.m. PT: CAB Lead or CAB executive to Summarize Key Inputs, Follow-Up Steps, Thank People, and Adjourn

In closing the meeting, take a quick poll: Did having a two-hour, virtual CAB meeting work best for everyone? I have received feedback from customers that two hours worked well for them, and they would be unwilling to do a half or a full day virtually. Be sure to check in with your CAB to get their input before closing out the meeting.

Explain to the customers that you and an executive will follow up with each customer. (This is bare minimum.) For more ideas on how to continue developing your relationship, see chapter 6.

Optional: Adding an Early Adopter Story by a CAB Customer

Invite a customer who was an early adopter to talk about their use cases and why they made the investment over the competitors. This customer should be eloquent and tie the product or service to their business needs. Adding this guest speaker would work best after the feature that prompted their investment is mentioned.

Accepting Feedback

Don't be overly concerned about negative feedback. However, the best CAB meetings—in-person, virtual, or hybrid—garner constructive negative feedback. This is what you and your company need to hear so you can create better experiences for your customers. There will always be a board member who wants to be heard. Even if you've done a one-to-one pre-call or sneak-peek call to prepare customers for the virtual experience, there will inevitably be at least one who complains about the format. There are just some people who like to voice their opinion.

Always remain cool and don't let the feedback get you down. Give the board customers space to be heard. If customers open up, take it as a sign you've created trust with your board. As the CAB lead, always offer to have a one-on-one meeting with any board member for follow up and let CAB customers know they will also have exclusive one-on-one time with a vendor executive. These opportunities help CAB customers feel truly heard and respected for their feedback.

Positive or negative, take in all the feedback. Follow up if you need more details and thank each board member. They took the time to share. It's on you to be sincere and responsive.

Pro Tip: Beware of overly positive feedback

Overly positive feedback often indicates the customer board member wants more access to company (vendor) executives, future discounts, opportunities to attend another CAB meeting, or to be invited to another VIP event.

CAB Meetings That Last Through Lunch

Inexperienced CAB leaders may want to stretch the meeting from morning to afternoon and skip the lunch break. Please get to know your customers before asking them to power through. If you're going to extend the meeting through lunchtime, give the board at least a fifteen-minute break. If you have the budget and it works for the customers attending virtually, give them a gift card for lunch.

Case Study: A Kickoff Virtual CAB Focused Only on Biotech Customers

The company's goal was to have one virtual CAB meeting for each vertical (industry) to understand the buyer personas and validate a vertical marketing strategy.

Challenge

This nimble B2B SaaS company wasn't sure if the biotech industry was where they should invest more research and development. They had a lot of success in winning new biotech start-up customers. However, the biotech sales cycle was longer than most. Sales and marketing were never sure who the key decision-makers were since they varied from customer to customer. This company was also seeking another round of funding to be a formidable competitor against the number one SaaS in their category. Having a CAB now, they suspected, would give them additional insights to improve their funding pitch deck and to decide whether to invest in more biotech-specific product features.

Solution

To bring all the potential decision-makers among the customers together in one place with the company's C-suite, sales and marketing created a virtual CAB for East and West Coast executives and customers. I was the CAB lead.

Planning and Replanning

While planning the CAB meeting, I learned that the product marketing manager was new and didn't have a great rapport with the product management lead. This became noticeable when the product management person wouldn't attend the pre-CAB content meetings when the product marketing person attended.

I couldn't fix the relationship between these two. Instead, I quickly pivoted plans for the CAB to focus on the newest biotech customers, whom neither the product management lead nor the product marketing manager had met. By focusing on new customers, there would be less friction between the teams as to who owned the relationship with the customers. Internally, everyone would be thrilled to meet their newest customers.

Inside the Virtual Biotech CAB

Since this was the company's first CAB ever, I created a two-hour CAB agenda. I invited the CEO, CTO, and CMO. The company was also in the process of hiring a CRO. Additionally, I invited two VPs from product management to present to the customers. There were ten people as panelists, including me. I also took on the CAB facilitator role, and I asked for a marketing manager in charge of webinars to help set up the virtual event. I asked other marketing members to take notes and observe speakers.

For the first CAB, I decided to ask less than ten customers to join. I typically like to have only six customers, but the executives said they really wanted more customers to participate. The leaders from this company didn't have a lot of experience attending or leading a CAB meeting, so I wanted everyone to focus. Having too many customers wouldn't be engaging. We ended up with eight customers who were selected because they were the decision-makers from mostly biotech start-ups with less than six hundred employees. They were a mix of titles—IT CIOs, managers, and heads of different business units. I invited the CSMs and sales support to attend the webinar as attendees. The CAB customers knew their CSMs and sales were attending.

Here's a walk-through of the agenda for the virtual biotech CAB meeting:

8:00–8:10 a.m.: Welcome from the CEO and a Review

The CEO's talk had no slides. It was very well received and warm. It helped set the tone of the CAB.

8:10–8:30 a.m.: Icebreaker: Share Your Live Music Experience to Open Up

All the members opened up. The icebreaker ran ten minutes overtime, but it had everyone engaged.

8:30–8:50 a.m.: Company Update by the CTO—Business Outlook and Where the Company Was Going

The customer board was engaged and excited. There were lots of smiles and nods. There were no follow-up questions, just acknowledgments of the outlook and health of the company.

8:50–9:20 a.m.: Product BioTech Roadmap

Two product leads presented the biotech roadmap. This was curated specifically for the biotech industry. In other words, they focused only on new R&D for biotech customers. First, they presented the roadmap and later a live demo. Customers hardly interrupted the roadmap presentation. The product leads had to pause and solicit feedback. A few CAB customers asked for the same demo to be given to their teams.

9:20–9:45 a.m.: Product User Interface and Onboarding

Product management asked the customers if there was value to their features, if their employees would need onboarding training, and if the user experience was positive.

The customers on the board were cautious about adopting the new features. They confided that they weren't immediately willing to try out the newest features or upgrade to the latest version.

A customer shared that due to their industry, they weren't willing to be beta testers and requested control over the upgrades. When asked why, they said they didn't want a deluge of support tickets from their employees, who would complain about why there wasn't training or notice of these new features. That was noted. Customer marketing needed to do a better job in communicating updates and adding knowledge base article links to email newsletters.

One of the cofounders shifted the discussion to decision-making. More than half the board mentioned that the head of finance or the CFO would make the final decision, and that it wasn't IT. The board suggested creating more content for a finance decision-maker. The lead product person acknowledged their feedback and asked to follow up with each customer board member. They mentioned on the follow-up calls that they wanted to dive deeper into what content would resonate with their head of finance or CFO to help them plan to sell to the main decision-makers in the biotech industry.

One hour and forty-five minutes in, the company knew who the decision-makers were for their newest customers and had a direct point of contact to approach regarding the new feature of the product.

9:45–9:55 a.m.: CMO Presentation of New Biotech Brand Strategy

The customers were shown the new biotech ads. They were pleasantly excited about the new brand ideas coming from the CMO. The CMO even asked if they would be willing to be quoted on a future billboard. Many nodded in approval.

9:55–10:00 a.m.: Summary, Follow-Up, Closing, and Thank You

I acknowledged the CAB customers' specific feedback, discussed what we needed to follow up on, and thanked them for their time (a total of two hours). I shared how the company team would prioritize their insights and feedback, and I would send out a follow-up in twenty-four hours. I said company executives were looking forward to having in-depth one-to-one conversations with them in the future.

Insights from the Biotech Industry CAB

At the post-CAB executive meeting, I asked for feedback on the virtual CAB meeting.

The C-suite saw, in real time and face-to-face, the value of meeting different decision-makers and hearing different perspectives from the customers. This helped all the company's leaders understand the biotech sales cycle. They now knew that they needed to be ready to win over a CFO. They, or their teams, made sure to follow up with the customers on the board to gain more detail on how to achieve that. One C-suite member shared that they weren't surprised by the board feedback but was glad that the company's leaders had heard the feedback directly from the customers.

Product leaders weren't surprised by the board not being willing to try the newest features and not wanting to upgrade to the latest versions. They were aware of the problem, but they had not tackled it. The CAB gave them confidence and the inspiration to do so. After that first CAB meeting, the product management leaders thought of creating a sandbox beta for the biotech CAB members. Now, product leads had access to new non-IT (business) leaders to help them design better user interfaces for workflows.

Product marketing learned firsthand why non-IT made purchasing decisions, which helped them update their sales and website content. The VP of product marketing asked to join the one-on-one board calls as an observer, so they could listen and create better CFO content to help speed up the buying process.

The CMO felt validated that their brand strategy was a timely investment against competition. The CMO gained additional respect from the other leaders and helped support their future vertical marketing initiatives, which showed that the benefits of the CAB extended beyond improving their relationship and strengthened internal company relationships.

Growth Learnings from the Virtual CAB: A Personal Perspective

As the CAB lead, I learned that I wore too many hats during the virtual CAB meeting. I was a front-of-house and behind-the-scenes moderator and a backend facilitator making sure the company's speakers were ready to take the stage.

I was used to running it all during an in-person CAB meeting. With technology (we used the Zoom One product for the CAB), I have learned it's best to separate the functions. Have a designated moderator and a separate facilitator during each virtual CAB session. At least I realized before it started that I needed help taking notes. I invited a product marketing person to do that. I had also realized that I needed help with the backend webinar solution, so I asked our video conference webinar operations person to be on standby during the live CAB meeting.

Feedback from CAB Customers

After the CAB, I followed up with many of the board members. Here's their candid feedback:

- One of the eight board members thought the icebreaker went on too long.

- More than 50 percent wanted the meeting to go longer.

- One member asked for a four-hour CAB, or half day with breaks, so they could check work emails or texts.

- Another customer said the executive recap slide at the end of the CAB was a little light on details, but they understood it was high level due to the sensitive material.

- Karl, one of the customers on the board, shared his feedback:

  For me, sitting on the CAB as a new customer helped me decide whether I should invest more in this SaaS or not. And now having access to the executives also gives me an advantage in ensuring more of a mutual relationship than being beholden by a vendor.

The Outcome: Mostly Soft Key Performance Indicators (KPIs)

Soft KPIs are another way to gauge whether the CAB was worthwhile and had substance for the customer advisory board member—first and foremost, did the customer build trust and mutual respect, and will they reciprocate to support this company. After the biotech CAB, customers did reciprocate, see below:

- The company asked CAB customers to speak at upcoming industry events and film a video.

- The company gained access to business personas to help learn CFO objections to develop sales and marketing content.

- Customers gained new networks outside of their peers. For example, a business line owner wanted to talk to another customer IT board member to get ideas on how to make an argument to increase training for end users and wanted a demo of their training software.

- More than half of the CAB customers asked to join the beta program if there was a sandbox environment. Even the less reluctant customer board members were eager to test and give feedback.

- Two board members asked to speak to the Professional Services team for a custom version of quality assurance workflows.

My Secret Sauce: Offer a Series of Virtual CAB Meetings

Instead of trying to cram two days' worth of information into a two- or three-hour virtual CAB, consider running a series of virtual meetings. It's extremely difficult to concentrate for three hours online. By running a series instead, a CAB lead can provide more time for customer feedback while keeping everyone engaged and focused. A series provides you with the best virtual CAB outcome, and you will not only meet your goals but exceed them. Depending on your goals, the series can be two to three meetings over the course of one to two months, and each meeting would be sixty to ninety minutes long. This will give you higher engagement and better outcomes while building trust among the CAB members.

I recommend a three-meeting series, with each meeting including these high-level sessions.

Series 1

Welcome, review agenda and series

Ice breaker: What is your most memorable vacation experience?

Company Update: Executives present what is going on in their company.

Discussion: Customers to ask questions about the company update.

Close: Summarize this meeting, follow up and mention next series.

For the second series, I've provided two options to show you how you can build your own CAB.

Series 2—Example focuses on Business Review

Welcome, review agenda

Review of the business: few slides to get people to talk about a specific topic. What executives have learned and what they are doing

Discussions

Forming solutions, actions

Assignment of who is taking the lead, get leader to acknowledge

Review next series

Session 2—Example focuses on Strategy Review

Welcome, agenda

Executive provides overview of strategies and what steps they are taking

Discuss strategy, but first have another executive add more "color." Ask each customer board member to give their input.

Prioritize feedback, actions, go deeper

Summarize: What are the next actions that the executive will take (one-on-one calls, offer to speak to the board member's team).

Close: Review next the last series, what roadmap features will they present

Session 3—Product or Service Roadmap

Welcome, agenda

Overview of the roadmap review

Feature one, two and three

Introduce the pay-for-features game

Discussions from the game

Customer feedback of the series

Close: Discuss follow up, thank them

Session 1 of the Virtual CAB Meeting Series

The first virtual board meeting should start with an icebreaker for the board to get to know each other. This is fun, but it takes up time. Icebreakers can take up to thirty minutes because you'll likely have six customers and six executives.

After the icebreaker, I suggest the company executive sponsor present a company overview update. The number one goal is to have the company open up to customers, to share more than what they would hear from their account representative. It's crucial to develop trust with your customers during the first meeting.

Next, review a priority topic. This could be a roadmap, challenges, and/or strategies that you want feedback from your board on. Provide ten minutes for customers to ask questions of the company executives. If the questions go over, great, you'll communicate all the next steps over email. As the CAB lead, have some CAB customer questions ready to ask if there's silence. When closing the meeting, be ready to speak to the high-level discussions, and especially mention what areas of feedback need to happen from the company side. For example, a customer may ask a question about professional services, and you'll have to get the head of Professional Services to follow up after the meeting. The main message of closing is: we heard you (you is the customer advisory board members), we listened, we acknowledged, and we will be following up to share how we fix, find, or solve the feedback given to us.

The first virtual CAB meeting is the start of developing trust with your board members, which will create excitement, interest, and higher engagement for the entire series, where the company executives can start to validate concerns/strategies and get sincere feedback from the customer board members.

Session 1 Agenda

Time 60–90 minutes	Action
5 minutes	Welcome, review agenda and series.
30 minutes	Ice breaker: What is your most memorable vacation experience?
10–25 minutes	Company Update: Executives present what is going on in their company.
10–25 minutes	Discussion: Customers to ask questions about the company update.
5 minutes	Close: Summarize this meeting, follow up, and mention next series.

CAB Lead Pro Tip: Encourage customer board members to network offline.

Between CAB meetings, ask executives to reach out to customer board members and have a video conference to keep solidifying connection and trust with your advisers.

In Between Virtual CAB Series Sessions: Keep Customers and Executives Prepared and Connected

After each meeting in the series, don't forget to follow up, even if it's just a short email reviewing what was covered and the next action items. To increase customer and executive engagement, ask each executive to schedule a fifteen- to thirty-minute follow-up call with a customer. This helps build a connection and rapport with each board member, and it will increase the chances of them speaking much more openly at the next CAB session. Make sure it's a one-on-one meeting and that executives are prepared by providing them with access to the Post-CAB Customer Dashboard/Profiles spreadsheet.

Suggest executives ask the customer the following questions on the call:

- What are your thoughts on the board meeting?
- What agenda topic(s) did you like?
- What piqued your interest about joining the CAB and why?

Ask the executives to jot down notes from the one-on-one meeting. This activity will provide a similar experience to a customer and executive having a sit-down lunch or hallway coffee-break conversation during an in-person CAB meeting.

Another way to keep customers and executives prepared is to ask the CSMs to help drive these calls. It's a great way to keep your CSMs tied to the CAB. However, it will lose some of that VIP feeling since the executive and the customer aren't connecting one-on-one. As the CAB lead, decide whether executives should set up the meeting or if you need to involve the CSMs.

Session 2 of the Virtual CAB Meeting Series

Depending on your company CAB goals, there are two options.

The first option is to have a business review—aka a deep dive into issues to validate strategies and/or understand buying habits.

Go with this option if your executives know the issues at hand inside their company. Often leaders have a couple of ways to fix issues, or executives want to get customer advisers' perspectives firsthand. There are some executives who may want to dive deep to find the root cause, discuss the issues, and come up with solutions with their board.

The second option is to vet a strategy.

Go with this option if your executives want to discuss a strategy or get a sense of what other solutions or products customers would buy from your company. Perhaps the COO isn't sure if they should start to build out a professional services (PS) organization to support enterprise installations, onboarding challenges, and custom engineering. The COO would want to validate with CAB customers if this would be a worthy investment because building out a PS organization would take time and be costly. The product marketing leaders often like to validate why customers make a purchase. They may want a session to conduct a focus group within the CAB to ask questions, such as how the customers describe the products to help with the company's SEO strategy, product positioning, and messaging.

Session 2 Agenda (with two options)

Option 1: Business Review—1 hour		Option 2: Strategy Review—1 hour–90 minutes	
Time	Action	Time	Action
5 minutes	Welcome, agenda	5 minutes	Welcome, agenda
15 minutes	Review of the business: few slides to get people to talk about a specific topic. What executives have learned and what they are doing.	15 minutes	Executive provides overview of strategies and what steps they are taking.
15 minutes	Discussions	40 minutes	Discuss strategy, but first have another executive add more "color." Ask each customer board member to give their input.
10 minutes	Form solutions, actions	20 minutes	Prioritize feedback, actions, go deeper
5 minutes	Assignment of who is taking the lead, get leader to acknowledge.	5 minutes	Summarize: What are the next actions that the executive will take (one-on-one calls, offer to speak to the board member's team).
5 minutes	Review the last of the series (roadmap).	5 minutes	Close: Review the last of the series, what roadmap features will they present.

Session 3 of the Virtual CAB Series

Session 3 should present the product or service roadmap and usually takes about two hours.

Be careful not to try to present the entire roadmap and a long list of features. Remember, a downside of a virtual CAB meeting is maintaining concentration. It's hard to keep your customers' focus and undivided attention with a lengthy and involved roadmap presentation. I recommend showing the roadmap, having an executive present on a few key high-level themes, and then sharing which elements of the roadmap will be the focus of the meeting and discussion. After the scheduled discussion time, show the roadmap again and ask the customers if there are other features they want to discuss.

The feedback from the Session 3 roadmap discussion can help identify discussion points for future virtual CAB meetings, or it can lead to a smaller spin-off meeting between one CAB member and the product lead.

Executive and CAB Lead Pro Tip: Make your roadmap engaging by asking customers to vote on features.

If there's excitement for upcoming features on your roadmap, ask the customers on the board to vote for the ones that excite them the most. If there's significant interest in one or two features, you may want to have another CAB meeting on those.

To maintain customer engagement after the product or service feature presentations, borrow my colleague Yoav's idea and give your customers' play money to buy features. Start by pricing each feature and then giving your customers a budget of play money. Encourage them to use all their play money and give them five to seven minutes to decide. If you see people starting to look up before the seven-minute mark, start the discussion sooner. Ask each board member to share what they would buy and why. It's always a fun exercise to learn why the customers would purchase and how they would deploy the products, services, and features in their companies.

You'll be able to gauge whether the CAB met the customers' expectations after the third series session. Be open to constructive feedback. You can gather feedback from customers in post-meeting one-on-one calls or a survey or by allocating fifteen minutes of the virtual meeting agenda for customer feedback of overall CAB series. Asking for feedback in front of the entire board shows that you truly respect the board's time and their influence and advice. Note that if you go this route, there will be some shy customers who won't speak up at the meeting but who may write or call you afterward.

As always, follow up with your customers post-CAB meeting and ensure they have access to your executives. For more tips and strategies on world-class post-CAB actions, see chapter 6.

Session 3 Agenda

Time	Action
5 minutes	Welcome, agenda
10 minutes	Overview and high-level roadmap review to highlight the release features the meeting will focus on
20 minutes	Feature one (expert speaker or chief product officer) and include discussion
20 minutes	Feature two (expert speaker or chief product officer) and include discussion
20 minutes	Feature three (new concept to dazzle, first time showing) (expert speaker or chief product officer) and include discussion
5 minutes	Introduce the pay-for-features game: $100 of play money, how much would you pay if you only had $100 budget (CAB lead or product presenter)
5 minutes	Customers list how they would spend their money in the chat
15 minutes	Discuss the customer's choices and budgets
Optional: 15 minutes	Customer feedback of overall CAB series
5 minutes	Closing—CAB sponsor executive, thank and mention post-CAB meeting follow-up with executive

Case Study: Using a Virtual CAB Framework to Achieve Change Management

During the height of the pandemic, I moved into a new role at the unified communication-as-a-service (UCaaS) company. I made a lateral move to join the customer experience team. This was a team of analysts who ran the net promoter score (NPS) customer surveys for the entire company. The team was charged with educating business unit leaders of their NPS scores and feedback from hundreds of thousands of customers. With 35 percent growth quarter over quarter, the team pulled free-form survey feedback and spotted issues that business units needed to focus on to increase customer satisfaction.

The customer survey feedback examples were often abbreviated customer comments such as:

Implementation setup was hard to understand.

I was frustrated with the entire setup process.

I was charged right away for the service, and my system wasn't even up and running.

And why are there so many taxes?

I thought I was only paying per seat.

With my background in CAB programs, I suggested that we form a customer experience council of internal directors, vice presidents, and senior managers. In a departure from the norm in setting up a CAB, I focused on the middle management leaders who rarely got to engage with customers like executives would at a CAB. I invited them to be the council's sponsors.

Pitching and getting people excited to join wasn't a problem. However, the customer marketing team felt that I had stepped on their turf. I understood their feelings since I had led the CAB program in the past at this SaaS platform company. Respecting their roles, I called for a meeting and explained we were discussing NPS feedback and digging deep into how to pinpoint the root causes so that mid-management could take ownership. The customer marketing team understood and asked that I provide them with updates, especially about who was on our council. I was using my past CAB experiences to drive connections with customers who gave us NPS detractor scores and who were often super administrators, not chief information officers.

Challenge

It was difficult to get managers to listen to customers. As we set up iterative meetings for the council, most invited managers signed up but failed to attend. They would claim a meeting conflict or apologize for being pulled into a crisis. I was passionate that if middle management could connect and hear customer feedback firsthand, they could pinpoint the issues and find solutions that would increase our overall customer satisfaction and reduce churn.

Solution

NPS survey results led us to establish councils addressing implementation, sales experience, and customer support.

Once we began to set up these councils, I went looking for eight to twelve customers to join for three months at a time. I didn't offer them anything fancy to participate and shared that this was a new initiative for our company. Each customer on the council had to attend three meetings once a quarter to hear how we were addressing the survey feedback and to have the chance to provide feedback directly to leaders of the business units. I dug through surveys and asked customer success managers to nominate customers who would give constructive feedback.

Next, I asked our managers to volunteer to present to the customer experience councils. Many managers were already optimizing their process, so many had presentations and clear plans for changes ready for the council. I have a lot of gratitude toward the leaders who stepped up to present to the council. These managers had something in common. They were all customer-obsessed leaders who were often frustrated with the high-level survey data and wanted to meet customers who were unhappy.

Additionally:

- Prior to the kickoff of the customer experience councils, I had an internal meeting to explain the program.

- Before inviting each manager to join, I asked them to share what issues they wanted to discuss with customers, rather than just letting the NPS survey data determine the topics to be discussed.

- I turned the second half of the virtual customer experience council meetings into an open discussion, asking the customer council what other topics we should address.

Inside the Virtual Customer Experience Council

The first council meeting was an hour long, and attendees included company vice presidents, directors, and senior managers. The customers selected to join the council were mostly IT managers or the administrators of the SaaS platform.

First Council Meeting

We first had a general kickoff meeting, where we shared some high-level projects that the company was working on to increase the customer experience. The last twenty minutes were kept intentionally free to ask customers what areas they thought we needed to focus on.

Second and Third Council Meetings

For the next two council meetings, I invited our leaders to present their own business case studies to the council.

Second Customer Experience Council Meeting: Focused on new customer onboarding concerns

11:00 a.m.–11:02 a.m.: Opening: Two customer experiences we are tackling today

11:02 a.m.–11:45 a.m.: Internal guest speakers (two customer presentations, leaving time for feedback and questions)

- Our director of customer support and operations presented the self-serve support system. This led to a customer willing to invite their IT team to give deeper input on the technical documentation.

- A support executive led a discussion on implementation. Several of the customers shared their frustrations about the use of offshore services that stuck to a script and sounded like robots.

11:45 a.m.–11:50 a.m.: Summary of findings and what ideas should be "parked" for now

11:50 a.m.–12:00 noon: Close with follow-up actions: communicate next steps and confirm one-to-one meetings

Third Customer Experience Council Meeting: Focused on reviewing previous issues and revisiting "parked" items

11:00 a.m.–11:20 a.m.: Opening: Review of the two issues from previous council meeting and the outcomes

- Technical documentation will be partnering with sales engineering to create more informative and clear documentation. Sales engineering will review and provide comments before documents are published.

- The support executive is creating a new training that includes testing each implementation engineer on how to facilitate an implementation without reading a script.

11:20 a.m.–11:45 a.m.: Visiting the "parked" idea: Review self-serve implementation step, providing feedback on instructional language and steps

- Head of self-service facilitates the discussion of the implementation web GUI design.

- Customers walk through the steps and ask clarifying questions, because the instructions are not clear.

- Real-time, council customers suggest clearer ways to explain the steps in simple terms for an office manager to complete the implementation step.

11:45 a.m.–11:55 a.m.: Visiting the "parked" idea: Best way to engage customers after they implemented

- The director of training reviews new training modules to help small-business owners turn on more complicated features to support inbound calls from customers.

- Customer on the council suggests packaging up modules for use cases on virtual receptionist, which was the number-one request for a training module.

11:55 a.m.–12:00 noon: Close with follow-up actions: communicate next steps, an optional webinar on the new training module on virtual receptionist

- Each customer from the council will receive a follow-up call to get their feedback.

Insights of the Customer Experience Council

Even though internal leadership liked the idea of joining the council, when asked to attend, many would give the excuse that they were busy or would delegate to their junior manager to present. That turned out to be fine. As long as there was a leader listening, following up, and taking action, we achieved our ultimate goal of having direct access to customers.

To work around the challenges, I decided to publish a newsletter to promote the councils to all the leaders. These newsletters started to motivate additional leaders to present. I also had an appreciation day for the internal teams who took the customer council's feedback and implemented actions based on it. I wanted to keep promoting how frontline managers and middle management/leaders were really making a difference in our customer experience.

I asked Jace, a customer who wanted help with his implementation, to share his experiences. Doing so opened a positive interaction and higher engagement between our teams and our council members. Here's what Jace, a director of technical support, shared:

I was managing the vendor relationship of this UCaaS and was pleasantly surprised to be nominated to the council by my customer success manager. During the council meetings, I shared my frustrations with the council, and I asked the head of implementations on the spot to take a follow-up call. Right after the council meeting, I jumped on another video conference with the implementation managers. The managers resolved the issues within forty-eight hours, and I gave them detailed constructive feedback to help them reduce operational steps. I impressed my skip-level manager by quickly resolving many of our implementation issues as a council member.

The Outcome: Hard and Soft KPIs

- Ninety percent of the customer experience council members' NPS scores increased by 50 percent. These customers became promoters.

- Many of the internal leaders who presented were promoted within a year. These leaders would take the customer input to ask for budgets to find solutions.

- Managers who presented developed their own customer experience council. Having forged relationships, they were able to have quick meetings to show customers their process and get real customer feedback.

- Customers enjoyed the fact that they were meeting people who were accountable at the council. They felt more empowered. They had access to management and their support tickets weren't lost in a black hole. Many of these tickets were also brought up within leadership and fixed based on recommendations from the customer experience council.

- Many of the council members took ideas and processes back to their own IT teams to help them scale their services.

- Council members were more open to taking sales reference calls and increasing their UCaaS investment.

World-Class Virtual CAB Meeting Tips

Use these tips based on my hard-earned experience to run a world-class virtual CAB meeting. I've made mistakes so you don't have to!

> 💡 *Tip: Presenters must have exceptional soft skills.*

Ask all presenters to increase their presentation soft skills. Ask them to:

- Make eye contact.

- Smile.

- Repeat a question before answering the question.

- Incorporate slight pauses within their presentation for the virtual audience to collect their thoughts.

- Prepare to seamlessly pivot to another topic. Being comfortable pivoting to another topic is a must in a virtual CAB meeting.

Before the first CAB, send out a housekeeping note to customers and company executives with a reminder about the importance of soft skills, not like a nagging parent but like a peer who wants to help each presenter communicate as effectively as possible.

> 💡 *Tip: Content has to be curated with the CAB meeting in mind.*

The meeting is not a sales presentation. This is important for in-person CABs, but it is especially relevant when it comes to virtual meetings given the limited amount of time.

First, think about your board audience. If your CAB customers are users and not business leaders, your content will be different. Most virtual CAB speakers will take a shortcut and take from their daily pitch deck. While this makes complete sense, you only have sixty to ninety minutes with your board. If they notice these are the same slides they have seen from a sales presentation, they will discount the CAB.

Take the time to create CAB meeting slides that build up to the questions and discussions you want to have during the meeting.

> **Executive and CAB Lead Pro Tip:** Remind executives to think through all the potential customer questions/objections and prepare responses.

In virtual CAB meetings, the cadence has to be smooth. Executives must be prepared for questions. An "ahhh, I dunno" response will be a letdown, and it makes it look like your company executives don't know what they're doing.

As the CAB lead, remind executives to be prepared for specific questions and objections. For example, if an executive is presenting a feature, a customer may remember when they were upset by a disruptive software update that added new features. As the presenter, the executive will have to be ready to respond. Encourage executives to think about ways to get ahead of it: Can they ask their support or operations teams to brief them on how they have found a solution to ensure the software update won't cause disruption, or even better, invite them to speak at the CAB? Being prepared shows that your company leaders are high functioning, collaborate with each other, and have the same goal to improve customer experience.

Prepare your notetaker (or better yet, notetakers, one for each section of the virtual CAB) by providing them in advance with the list of likely questions/objections the executives have compiled for their presentations, so they can focus on jotting down any notes on these topics during the meetings or live discussion. You can also use a video transcription service, but I prefer that a human takes notes. It helps to have someone observing, listening, and recording voice inflections, facial movements, and other elements a transcript can't take into account.

🔅 Tip: Give Gifts to Virtual CAB Members

If your budget is limited, ask your events team to supply gifts from their budget. Partner with your events team, because they will need customers to speak at their upcoming events. With this partnership, you and the events team can preplan which customers from the CAB can support future go-to-market events.

I feel strongly about showing gratitude through thoughtful gift-giving. For more on how to thank customers, see chapter 3, page 60.

🔅 Tip: Plan for What You'll Do If the Meeting Goes Overtime

During the virtual meeting, the CAB lead should be minding the time. If there's good feedback and dialogue, let it keep running, just not excessively. If the roadmap creates high engagement, you'll have two choices.

- Stick to the schedule. You'll have to step in, politely interrupt, and transition to the next session. Ask customers to stay another fifteen to thirty minutes after the scheduled close of the virtual meeting to continue the discussion. In my experience, most customers don't book back-to-back meetings next to a CAB meeting. If more than 10 percent of the board can't stay, then reschedule another short meeting for the next day.

- Keep the conversation going until the end of the virtual meeting. There will be no closing. If this happens, the CAB lead needs to say there will be a follow-up email to discuss future CAB logistics.

Chapter 7 covered the following:

- Reasons for having a virtual CAB, and how to overcome challenges you may face running a virtual CAB.

- Best practices on how to run a virtual CAB that will create an engaging and positive experience for customers and executives.

- Why a series of virtual CAB meetings is the best way to cover several hours' worth of information and achieve your company's goals.

The lack of face-to-face interactions in a virtual CAB is one of its biggest drawbacks. The next chapter will cover how you can get the best of both in-person and virtual CABs with a hybrid CAB.

8
HOSTING A WORLD-CLASS HYBRID CAB

A hybrid CAB approach gathers the entire board together in both in-person meetings and virtual meetings. It is not a meeting to which you invite people to be in a physical location and invite others who can't travel to join over a video conference platform. With a hybrid CAB approach, everyone on the board meets together whether it's in-person or virtual. In most cases, the first CAB event is in-person and follow-up discussions are held virtually.

As I am sure you've gathered, I believe strongly in the value of in-person CAB meetings, but I have come to believe the best CAB programs are hybrid. The hybrid approach provides the best of both worlds: in-person relationship building with ongoing virtual connection. Discussions started at the in-person meeting can continue over a virtual meeting. Executives can follow up and discuss what actions they have taken, ask the board for more help, and have customers bring topics to discuss. The virtual CAB acts as an "all-together" action for the board to connect, advise, and build upon the physical CAB meeting.

To execute a hybrid CAB approach, you now have the foundation to build as a CAB lead or host as a CAB executive sponsor an in-person CAB (in chapter 3), virtual CAB (in chapter 7), and post-CAB sponsorship program (in chapter 6). In this chapter, you'll learn some more best practices as well as two case studies that illustrate the opportunities and challenges of going hybrid.

The Four Benefits of a Hybrid Approach

1. **Flexibility:** Hybrid meetings offer unparalleled flexibility for your business when it comes to creating your CAB at any inflection point in your company. A hybrid CAB program provides more access to your CAB customers, giving you more time to build long-standing relationships that provide you with more opportunities to validate and ask questions of your board members.

2. **Cost savings:** By reducing the need for travel and accommodation, businesses can save money on expenses related to physical meetings. This includes airfare, hotels, and conference room rentals.

3. **Reduced environmental impact:** Fewer in-person meetings mean fewer carbon emissions from travel, which can contribute to your company's sustainability goals.

4. **Increased productivity:** Virtual meetings often require more structured agendas and shorter durations, potentially leading to more focused and productive discussions.

Reasons for Moving to a Hybrid CAB

Clients will often want to strategize when and where to have a CAB. I love this time with clients; they're excited and have so many goals. Many executives I speak with want a hybrid CAB to combine internal efforts and budgets.

For example, a chief marketing officer (CMO) reached out and told me they have decided to partner with the chief revenue officer (CRO) to run a CAB. Their goal was to make a big splash at RSA World, an IT security industry conference, and get their customers to add a few extra days after the end of the conference to attend the CAB meeting. They wanted to combine a CAB with the user conference to maximize the venue and time with customers and have them speak at the conference, join dinners to close deals, and speak to press and analysts. Then two to three weeks after the in-person CAB meeting, the CMO and CRO would follow up with the CAB customers over a virtual conference system. In the end, they decided it was too expensive to have a CAB event at the conference and decided to focus on meeting customers to see who would be an appropriate fit to join their CAB. They brought me in to plan their in-person CAB in the fall and to continue having virtual CAB meetings into the new year.

Adding a CAB meeting to an industry conference makes complete sense, but keep in mind your customers may not see it as a great idea and decline to join. Why? Your customers are taking time to attend an industry conference so they can learn and listen to other experts and peers about industry topics. These customers may have closer relationships with other vendors and peers and will likely support the other vendors' dinners and analysts and press requests. PR and analyst requests could include taking your customers to dinner, meeting at a conference, having a Zoom meeting with an industry analyst, or allowing your head of PR to work with their public relations firm to pitch the customer's use case story to technical and industry media outlets. You haven't established a connection between you and your customers yet, so there is also the risk that by asking them to extend their trip (basically asking them for a favor), your customers will feel taken advantage of. This not only will sink the CAB, it could decrease their brand loyalty in their minds and checkbooks.

Adding a CAB in-person meeting to a company user conference is a little different. A user conference is sponsored by a company, has a smaller footprint, and has strategic partners who aren't competitors. If your company has a user conference, you won't be competing with other vendors for customers' time. Note that RSA World and Amazon Web Services (AWS) conferences started out as user conferences, but they created a large ecosystem and these conferences turned into industry events where competitors purchase event space.

Having a CAB meeting at your conference could work in your favor. Josh, the product strategy leader from chapter 1, shares his CAB meeting experience during their yearly user conference.

We hold a CAB before our annual user conference, and it's great getting intimate time with our customers. Then throughout the conference, we can have smaller one-to-one conversations where the CAB members may feel comfortable sharing details with me that they wouldn't in a group setting. It's all about relationships and trust.

Josh has been to over 150 CABs. I also led an all-flash storage CAB for him, so I take his experience seriously. Here Josh points out how having the CAB before the user conference allowed him to develop a more human connection with his board members throughout the conference.

On the flip side, the conference is also time bound and there's only so much free time to reconnect during the conference. Executives also have to juggle their time meeting other customers who flew in from far destinations and weren't invited to the prestigious CAB, along with making time to meet media and industry analysts in person. However, after meeting your customers in person you've gained enough familiarity and connection to host a successful virtual meeting in the near future, either a deeper dive into relevant topics during one-on-one videoconferences or with the entire board for thirty to sixty minutes.

It is possible to have the in-person CAB component at a user conference, however it needs to be planned with the conference event team leads.

Case Study: An EMEA CAB Moved to a US User Conference and Kept the Connection Going by a Virtual CAB Beta Testing Program

Background

A US-based vendor held a yearly SaaS user conference in the United States, typically slated for super administrators to maximize their investment. Mostly US and Canadian customers attended. I ran the customer advocacy program and had a customer advocacy manager with no CAB experience on my team.

Challenge: Six Weeks to Plan an In-Person CAB Meeting

Although the company was growing, the executives asked many budgets to be cut to support R&D. Marketing had to cancel a CAB meeting held in Europe for Europe, Middle East, and Africa (EMEA) customers.

EMEA sales leadership pushed back. They argued that their European big-brand customers needed to feel confident about the US-based company. That was why the CAB program had been expanded to other regions. They insisted on the benefits of an EMEA CAB and argued for it to take place during the user conference in the United States. The EMEA CAB meeting and the user conference would surely encourage its top customers not only to become advocates but to have confidence in making future investments with the SaaS platform.

Solution: Eight EMEA CAB Customers Attended the US User Conference

There was some initial resistance from executives to the EMEA sales leadership's request because it sounded more like they were offering a vacation to customers than a board meeting. There were also only six weeks to plan and multiple other mini programs happening within the user conference, such as a CIO roundtable, an analyst relation dinner, and strategic partners meetings. The conference and resources were stretched.

Since I ran the customer-speaking desk and was in charge of keynotes, executive panels, and general breakout sessions that needed customers, I asked the EMEA sales leadership team to nominate four to five EMEA CAB customers to speak at our US conference. Having at least that number of EMEA customers speak at the conference would help our global brand, especially during keynotes and executive panels.

I ran the numbers and pointed to the savings made by having the EMEA CAB during the US yearly user conference. Budget-wise, the user conference had secured excellent hotel room rates. Conference space was easier to obtain and cost-effective. We saved money by inviting the customers to the United States and not needing to fly at least eight executives from the US to a CAB in Europe.

The US-headquartered executives would be at the user conference, so they would strengthen their relationships with the EMEA customers. The EMEA customers would get to network with other customers outside their region, attend conference sessions, and meet many of our subject matter experts in person.

The C-suite approved the EMEA CAB six weeks before the conference. I knew there was a high risk of failure in such a tight workback: there were so many things that could go sideways. Internally, the customer advocacy manager wanted to take responsibility for this CAB. While I felt this wasn't the best time to have an inexperienced manager oversee a CAB, I knew if I gave her a template, she would be able to run the CAB meeting smoothly.

We invited a British chief technology officer, who had attended our CAB meeting the previous year in Monterey, California, to be the EMEA CAB ambassador. His role was to connect his new CAB peers to the company's executives and subject matter experts during the user conference. Additionally, the CTO was a natural facilitator. We asked if he could help lead one or two CAB discussions. Having a veteran CAB customer on the board wasn't just insurance; it was a must for me. Having a board advocate speak to the value of the CAB and their willingness to serve on our board shows new customer board members how established our customer board is and that we invest time in deepening our relationships with customers.

Outcome: EMEA Customers Built New Connections with Company Executives and Peers Outside of Europe

Typically, in-person CAB meetings happen over the course of two and a half days. This CAB meeting would be different in that it was shorter, because it was a last-minute add-on.

First, we would host a wine tasting and dinner off-site and host the CAB meeting the next morning. The board meeting would only be three hours long, and the CAB agenda was tailored specifically for the EMEA customers to get a better sense of our subject matter experts.

The EMEA customers met at Heathrow Airport in London to take the same flight to San Francisco. Because of strict European Union gift policies, many customers had to pay for their own flight. However, we paid for their hotel and entertainment.

When they arrived at SFO, we shuttled everyone to the San Francisco user conference hotel. The next day, they had a day trip to Napa for a wine tasting and an Italian seafood dinner in Sausalito, overlooking the Golden Gate Bridge at sunset.

Once the word was out that the top EMEA customers were going to Napa for a day of wine tasting, many of the company's leaders were keen to join them. Because of the budget cuts, we had to be prudent and set up a limited "chaperone arrangement," aka an executive sponsorship program, with follow-up responsibilities. Each executive who went to Napa had to be an EMEA customer sponsor for a year, which meant the EMEA customer would have a US leader as their company sponsor to support their customer needs for one year.

We did everything possible to maximize the impact of the EMEA customers' presence. One CAB customer was invited to be a keynote speaker, another was a guest speaker at the CIO roundtable event, and another customer joined us for a main stage customer panel, which helped us reiterate our growth in Europe.

The EMEA CAB meeting held during the user conference was a sales team success. During the three hours, we focused on one priority topic: how we dealt with data and privacy in Europe to comply with European Union law and policy. The board customers felt much more confident in investing in the platform than going with an established enterprise platform because they had made a personal connection with the company.

Their CAB experience, the conference sessions, and networking with many American and Canadian fellow customers helped the EMEA customers validate back to their HQ that this SaaS platform was worth investing in to meet their needs.

When we extended our invitations to the EMEA customers to join our CAB, we had made it an up-front requirement that each customer would be a beta tester in EMEA. We told them that the beta would not only help our company, but it would help theirs too. We committed to providing extra free resources to CAB members during beta testing. This turned out to be a boon for the company.

Keeping the EMEA CAB Going

We kept the EMEA CAB going with virtual CAB meetings centered around the beta testing. This allowed our US-based company to have consistent dialogue with our EMEA CAB customers.

The beta program for the EMEA CAB was a positive post-CAB benefit that helped us develop early adoption in Europe. Additionally, many board members helped us locally in Europe by speaking at launch events, to press, in videos on location, and to European analysts and customers.

These virtual CAB meetings turned into a very tactical way to keep our US leadership in touch with our EMEA customers.

Lessons Learned

I realized that before the EMEA CAB, the company should have created an executive sponsorship program. This would have allowed the US executives to spend more time with the EMEA customers at the user conference. As it was, the customers didn't meet the executives beforehand, so their willingness to open up was abbreviated due to the demands of attending the user conference.

Because the actual CAB meeting was only three hours long, with a lunch off-site to make their visit an experience, the connections made weren't as deep as in other in-person CAB events. There was little in-person time compared to the length of a typical CAB meeting, which could last for at least eight to ten hours over the course of two and a half days.

In hindsight, the CAB content was lackluster. Due to the simultaneous user conference, the product marketing and product management teams were overwhelmed. Their responsibility was to build unique content for all the conference sessions, so much of the CAB content suffered. Luckily, the European customers weren't that upset with the CAB content because they appreciated that we focused on specific EU law and regulation around data and privacy. This acknowledged that we understood European customers have different needs and showed how we met those needs. And our customer advocacy manager created a special VIP experience for our customers.

Due to the concurrent user conference sessions, there was less time for executives and European customers to spend together. It was hard to have deeper discussions at the event. It wasn't a miss for our EMEA sales leadership team, but it was for me.

We also could have done a better job of adding more CAB virtual meetings, but our small team of two could only handle having CAB meetings for beta testing.

We could have done more to help each EMEA customer develop a deeper connection with executives.

We should have thought more about the practical impact of a concurrent user conference: it's hard to get the C-suite to attend a CAB during a conference. They will think their priority is to be seen by a greater number of people. We could have worked more closely with the events team and executive assistants to maximize the time for company executives and CAB members to connect.

It was invaluable to be crystal clear with the company executives' role with regard to interacting with each CAB customer. They knew going in that if the executive became a CAB sponsor, they would have to follow up with a quarterly video conference call.

Gareth was one of our EMEA CAB members who had joined our previous year's CAB. At the time, he was a CTO of a well-known IT consulting firm in London.

I served on the CAB for a total of two consecutive years. With no preconceived expectations for the first CAB, my objectives were to meet their C-suite and understand their plans for growth in Europe. For that first EMEA CAB during the US user conference, I took on more of an ambassador role than simply an advisory board member, helping to connect the new European customer to the executives and experts, leveraging the connections and relationships I'd made in the intervening period and facilitating discussions during the CAB. I was especially keen to help other EMEA peers feel welcome and to ensure that the content was tailored for the European board members such that we all benefited.

Case Study: From a Failing In-Person CAB Meeting to a Successful Virtual One

This case study is about how a company gracefully accepted defeat and turned a failing physical CAB into an engaging virtual CAB that, in turn, boosted a product launch with two Fortune 500 customers.

Background

The product manager wanted to have a CAB meeting at an analyst data center conference in Las Vegas to raise awareness of and gain feedback on a new product. So, our sales executives made introductions to their customers attending the conference. Many were Fortune 500–ranked customers. I gained access to these customers by offering exclusive first access to the beta version of the product. This meant these CAB customers would have a VIP beta experience, leading to upsell opportunities for each salesperson.

Challenge: Four Weeks to Get Fortune-Ranked Customers to Join Our CAB

Timing: We had four weeks before the conference to prepare for the CAB program. The programming was lengthy and tight. Most customers didn't want to fly in early or stay later for the CAB meeting.

Incentives: Incentives weren't an option to encourage customers to spend extra time at a CAB. Many of these Fortune-ranked customers couldn't accept vendor gifts.

Outcome: The CAB Was a Flop

There was no real solution to overcoming the constraints, but despite the lack of flexibility, twelve customers confirmed they would join the CAB. (All were new customers to me.)

I had identified a narrow window when we could hold the CAB meeting, right after the closing keynote. I booked a conference room just outside the hotel conference center and filled it with light snacks. To make it easy for customers to join us, I made sure the board meeting would be as close as possible to the conference's closing keynote session.

The 90-Minute CAB Aborted After 50 Minutes and Provided an Important Lesson

This is what happened. Most customers were tired and unable to focus at the CAB meeting. The product manager was both tired and nervous. He wasn't on his game. Thirty minutes into the meeting, the energy in the room was sinking. Fast. I scanned the customers' dull looks. I asked for a quick five-minute break, suggesting people could check whether their flights were on time. I pulled the product manager aside and asked him to wrap it up.

Everyone perked up as soon as we announced we were going to shorten the CAB meeting.

Solution: Pivoting to a Virtual CAB

I closed the CAB meeting and thanked everyone for attending after a long three-day stint at the conference and, since I was the marketing person, I told them we planned this ad hoc CAB because of a big launch that would be happening soon. I offered the CAB customers the snacks in the room, urging them to take them all for their flights.

Last, knowing it was important to get their permission before they left the room, I asked if we could have a follow-up video conference to discuss the new product with the CAB. They all agreed that would work.

After all the CAB members left, I had a wrap-up meeting with the product manager. He apologized and confessed he had stayed out too late the night before. I asked him to walk me through his entire presentation, and I found he had three more questions he wanted to ask the CAB customers to help him be launch-ready. I told him that since we were flipping to a web meeting, we should stick to a sixty-minute slot and would only be able to discuss two questions. He was upset and couldn't understand why we shouldn't block ninety minutes out of the customers' schedules. I felt we failed at the event, and that having a ninety-minute virtual CAB meeting would likely not get all the CAB members to attend, let alone excited to advise. I said I would consider it.

On my flight home, I racked my brain on how to accommodate the product manager's request. I couldn't. Ninety minutes was too much to ask of the customers. We had messed up in Las Vegas. I wanted to smooth things over by showing my respect for their time.

Back in the office, I focused on persuading six customers from the CAB to be beta testers, and I hoped that, from this pool, two board members would support our launch publicly.

That same week, I set up a one-to-one meeting with the product manager, which I led since I was in charge of the CAB. I told him we would have a sixty-minute web conference with twelve customers, and instead of allowing the product manager to pick the two topics to discuss, I asked him to write up all three topics as CAB discussions. These were to be high-level discussions in order not to expose the launch details.

Next, I emailed the twelve CAB members the three topics and asked each of them to rank them in order of importance for discussion. By doing that, the product manager now had an idea of what was most interesting to the CAB members. Customers interested in the third most popular idea could schedule a one-to-one at their convenience, or if there was enough interest, it would be easy to schedule a further meeting.

Then I circled back with an outline for the web meeting:

Data Center: High-Level Roadmap

- Topic 1—presentation and discussion
- Topic 2—presentation and discussion
- If time permits, Topic 3
- Next steps and closing

I added the teaser to Topic 3, just to get everyone excited. It was always possible someone would bring up that topic to discuss, now that it had been mentioned in the agenda.

The product manager was supportive once I explained why the virtual CAB needed to last only sixty minutes. There was no more debate about pushing out the CAB to ninety minutes.

We didn't get to Topic 3 during the virtual CAB meeting. I closed with offering an executive summary of the meeting and told the members we would follow up individually to assess if they would like to continue to be on this board.

After the virtual CAB meeting, I wrote up the discussion and shared it on a document showing the watermark "Confidential" to remind board members they had signed a mutual NDA for the CAB. I thanked them and said I would set up a thirty-minute one-on-one for their CAB feedback and to review the beta program to see if they would be interested in joining.

By racking up the customer cues and responses, I knew who would support us with a mini case study, join as a future beta tester, and likely be our VIP customers for our launch.

I asked each customer for a mini case study so I could get their approval for their high-level story. Fortune 500 companies are risk averse, and it can take five months to get a case study approved. There are instances when a vendor's CEO engages directly with a customer CEO, then approvals can be sped up in days. Getting the case study rolling with a lighter story, with few to no metrics, provides an opportunity for a case study to be approved. In the future, the Fortune 500 customer may beta test a product, and later we could have a higher chance of getting a launch quote approved, since the customer reviewer team had already approved a case study for us. And if not, we would still have a Fortune 500 customer story to add to our case study library.

I set up the pre-beta calls for the product manager. I was the moderator, and it allowed me to watch the interaction and gauge excitement when the customer was having a one-to-one with the product manager about the beta features. This helped me focus on who would be the best beta candidate to ask to support us during our product launch, and it gave me insight into what aspects of the product the customer was most enthusiastic about and would likely support us in.

The Beta and the Launch: Five Beta CAB Customers and Two Fortune 500 Launch Customers

We secured five beta customers from the original CAB, falling just short of my internal goal to find six. However, out of this pool, two Fortune 500 customers agreed to support the launch in the fall, which made management happy. With a combination of tact, respect, and drive, we had turned a dull and failing in-person CAB meeting into an exciting virtual one that enabled the product manager to build one-on-one relationships during the beta. Come launch time, many of the CAB Fortune-ranked customers' policies restricted them from supporting the launch, so only two out of the five could openly share, but we were grateful for that.

One customer traveled and spoke at two launch events: one was a local city event and the other was at a storage conference in New York City.

The second customer wasn't willing to travel or allow us to film a video on their campus. I knew the customer was shy, an introvert and incredibly astute. I asked our head of analyst relations (AR) if they were going to invite any technology analysts to do a white paper and webinar. It's typical to engage a third party to write their own analysis paper to critique a new product. And, yes, the AR team was looking for a beta customer to support their white paper and webinar.

I asked this second customer, who didn't want to travel or film, if he would like to speak to a well-known analyst to contribute to the white paper. I shared a recent research paper to show the quality of these publications.

I offered him three benefits:

- Access to a superstar industry analyst to build a relationship with them through one-on-one calls to help shape the white paper

- Exposure, as an expert in the published analyst paper, and as a guest speaker on the analyst webinar

- A free one-hour consultation with the analyst

The customer agreed and enjoyed the opportunities. He shined, especially on the webinar, and later his CAB and beta launch experience helped him get promoted. In the end, the customer wanted to reciprocate by offering to help in any future beta program.

A Hybrid CAB Can Support Your Company's Biggest Initiatives

If you aren't sold on running a hybrid CAB by now, let me emphasize: a hybrid CAB program can validate your customer strategies and help your company successfully launch new products and services. Here's how.

Every company wants to launch their new products or services with at least one customer story. Having more launch customers would prove more customer use cases of their product across different industries and company sizes and boost their marketing and sales initiatives.

Having an in-person CAB component allows your executives to easily ask customers what they think about the product, and it's easier to pick up physical cues and energy from one another. They can ask in real time what customers think about the product. These technical discussions and how the product may be used in the customer's environment will form a deeper partnership between the customers and executives. This time with customers is crucial. The CAB board will be connecting, listening, and reading each other's body language, and the back-and-forth banter will solidify trust. Once trust is formed, asking customers to support their launch as a beta tester or having early access to the product won't be seen as a favor to the vendor, but as an honor for the customers on the board. These in-person connections will ensure customers make it a priority to support your timely launch.

After the in-person CAB ends, pivoting the CAB to virtual meetings fosters these valuable connections. The product leader will lead product updates and share confidential product demos that the CAB members requested, or the head of product will ask customers for feedback on newest enhancements to the product. Note that there will be some board customers who may not become beta customers but can still be fantastic at giving feedback before a product launch.

By meeting in person and then having continuous virtual CAB meetings right up to and before the launch ensures that the product will be well received by the public. These virtual meetings can also help fuel the internal launch team such as product marketers, content storytellers, SEO experts, social media managers, CSMs, training and support teams. The launch team members will get to hear firsthand what customers are saying about the new product. These customer board voices and company use cases will motivate your launch team, so it is not only effective but surpasses KPI launch goals, and, more important, boosts your brand and company team culture.

Okay, now that I've convinced you that you need to get your executives on board with a hybrid CAB approach rather than strictly virtual, I've got you covered. (Pssst, copy these points into your presentation deck and please cite this book as your reference.) It comes down to this: the importance of face-to-face interaction. It's essential to have your executives meet your CAB customers in person because those meetings:

- **Build relationships:** Face-to-face meetings help build trust and stronger relationships among your customer advisory board members.

- **Allow them to read nonverbal communication:** Physical meetings allow participants to pick up on nonverbal cues like body language and facial expressions, which are often crucial to building trust and human connection.

- **Foster creativity and innovation:** Collaborative brainstorming and ideation sessions are productive when conducted in person.

World-Class Hybrid CAB Tips for the CAB Lead

When planning a hybrid program, always keep the world-class CAB principles in mind and this hard-won wisdom.

Plan Six Months in Advance

A world-class CAB requires planning, and that means allocating at least six months to get organized before the CAB meeting. Remember my Ad Hoc CABs Flop case study (page 217)! Take my advice and don't set yourself up for failure and dig yourself into a career hole because you didn't take the time to plan properly. If you are being pressured from your management to accelerate the schedule, use the information in this book to help you advocate for sufficient planning time.

Friends don't let friends run last-minute CABs (my new bumper sticker).

Chapter 8 covered the following:

- A hybrid CAB is where participants meet at in-person meetings and virtual meetings.

- Benefits and reasons for having a hybrid CAB, such as saving on travel costs by meeting in person at a conference and then continuing the CAB with virtual meetings.

- Examples of how I conducted a hybrid CAB format to help you plan your own.

CONCLUSION
A CAB IS ALL ABOUT
HUMAN CONNECTION

Intellectual property comes from the imagination, creativity, and minds of people, not from machines. —Jerry, a CEO of a network hardware and software company

This quote has been a mantra of mine when developing a CAB program. I want to share a few more words from Jerry:

At a CAB, customers and executives come together to deepen the imagination, harness the creativity that forms new human connections, and form a partnership founded on reciprocity.

CABs bring people together with intention. After building trust and exchanging ideas, a bond is created. Board members connect and openly share. It's like a jam session, where the CAB members can raise new ideas, questions, and objections and generate innovative solutions. The company is stirred to action because of the human connections made over the course of the CAB meetings.

Aha Moments

There are six different points during an in-person CAB—in the morning, during breaks, during and after lunch, during dinners, in one-on-one meetings, and after the board meeting when you reach out to your CAB members—that I refer to as "aha moments," or opportunities to create or deepen human connection.

If cultivated, these aha moments are the difference between achieving the current and future goals of your business and letting them slip through your fingers. The CEO who wanted to sit next to customers who had Latin American offices during the CAB lunch to help launch the company's expansion is a good example of cultivating an aha moment.

When you are the CAB lead, you're looking to create and help board members optimize these timely and strategic moments. If you are part of a CAB meeting, either as part of the planning or executive team, I encourage you to maximize these moments for yourself and for others in the room.

Morning

The CAB morning agenda is intense. Company executives are sharing confidential information and customer board members may nod while keeping a poker face because they aren't sure how to digest all the information given to them. Some customers may wonder if they can ask a question or if they should just take in the information. Customers have their first aha moment when executives not only share confidential information but do it in a way that shows sincerity and authenticity, perhaps even vulnerability if the executives are a little nervous during their presentations. Now customers feel more comfortable. They have empathy for the executives; and this feeling confirms for them why they were selected to serve as a customer adviser and builds trust.

For instance, I've been in two CAB meetings where we openly shared that we were filing for an IPO. The IPO news opened the trust phase. Customers immediately felt trusted and respected with such exciting news. Executives around the board table watched like hawks to get a read on the board's thoughts. The leaders were hungry for customer validation. A CAB is probably the first time the executives can get input directly from a group of customers.

Breaks

A break is a great time for a customer to find an executive who really piqued their interest during the morning session or for an executive to seek out a customer. It's also time for members to reconnect with a peer. Taking time for small talk also reinforces the CAB as a trusted and safe space so members feel encouraged to voice their opinions.

During and After Lunch

Customer advisers and company executives can banter freely while breaking bread. Smiles and hand gestures move gracefully around the room. People connect. By this time, trust and respect have deepened and relationships start to form as the board collectively imagines, creates, and intellectually solves together. After lunch, there's a shift: the board will start to ask difficult questions. Customers will dive deeper into the root of the issues to help the company come up with solutions because they care. It's a wonderful afternoon. People overall are comfortable and more authentic.

Dinner

Dinner is when everyone can relax after a long day. A CAB meeting is taxing not only on your intellect, but your emotional intelligence. There are typically some refreshments to get everyone to loosen up, because the day has been long. Imagine the energy it takes to join a CAB, not really knowing any of the other board members personally, and having to share confidential information and help solve problems and/or suggest ideas all day? Dinner is more relaxed and casual, safer. At the end of the day, trust is now present among the board members. Your customer board members are more likely to open up to your executives. The CAB company executives should be poised to ask customers questions or get their perspective on the CAB presentations.

One-on-One Moments

Another aha moment happens in the one-on-ones between a customer and an executive. At every board, a customer or an executive comes with questions they don't feel comfortable bringing up during the board meeting. Depending on the agenda, they will ask someone they feel can give them an authentic answer to meet up for a walk or get a cocktail off-site. This aha moment is to seek the truth. There's something about a CAB meeting that makes people want to pull people aside to talk. They want to know *why*, *what*, and *how*. It's also the start of truly connecting, forming not just respect but a lifelong reciprocal relationship.

After a CAB Meeting

The aha moments continue after the CAB meeting through the follow-up calls and video conferences. Even a simple text check-in could lead to learning something new for each person on the call. There will be a time when executives want to run things by customers. It can be anything—even personal—like asking the board member about their family trip to Cambodia or asking the CAB customer firsthand what they think of the new company partnership that was announced. Do they see the value? There are so many opportunities to be had between a customer and an executive. Many of them have even developed friendships from being on a CAB.

Your Time Is Sacred

The amount of time we spend on this Earth is quite short. What moves our heart and brain is human connection. Have you noticed people follow through on favors and go out of their way to help people they feel a connection to? It's the same at work.

Everyone's time is precious. If you are a CAB lead or an executive at a company, you'll be in overdrive overseeing, strategizing, attending meetings, taking in feedback, and balancing family time. Having CAB customer connections can help advance your career because you'll be able to draw on a group of trusted advisers to troubleshoot problems or share new ideas.

Unlock that power of human connection by hosting world-class CAB events and maximize it by having in-person CAB meetings or including an in-person component as part of a hybrid approach. Know that even if the goal of your CAB is to solve one problem or validate one strategy, the benefits will extend far beyond, for both the company and you, personally. Your CAB will foster more human connection for you to do your best and most fulfilling work. I hope this book has provided the inspiration and practical knowledge to create special connections you'll value and put into practice for the rest of your life.

APPENDIX
WORLD-CLASS CAB
RESOURCES

I've gathered blank templates of the spreadsheets and other planning tools used throughout the book on my website. Go to **www.ireneyam.com/book/world-class-cab-templates** to download them, or **scan the QR code**. Here's a list of what's available:

- Company Executive Sponsor's Involvement by CAB Stage Workback Template
- CAB Customer Dashboard/Profiles Template
- Mapping CAB Goals to the Agenda Template
- 3-Day In-Person CAB Agenda Time Allotment
- Post-CAB Dashboard/Profiles Template
- Post-CAB Dashboard/Profiles with Account Information Template (Prep for Quarterly Follow-Up Calls)
- Mapping CAB Goals to the Agenda Template
- Virtual CAB Communication Calendar

- Two-Hour Virtual CAB Meeting Agenda Template
- Virtual CAB Series Templates

AUTHOR'S NOTE

In this book, I've cited people by their first names only. Because of the private and confidential discussions that happened during and after the CAB programs, it would not be right to openly share further details.

Additionally, Simon the Pissed-Off Customer and Jon the Account Rep are two real examples that I anonymized. I wanted to respect these professionals, and their stories are not here to hurt them but for us to learn from how we are human.

ACKNOWLEDGMENTS

Back in 2019, I picked up Dave Kerpen's *The Art of People*, and it transformed me. Later, I was fortunate to meet him over a Zoom. Our meeting about being vulnerable sparked a new creative energy. After the pandemic, I found purpose and passion in CABs, and I wanted to make a stance that CABs can be one of the most memorable experiences in our careers. Today more than ever, we need more human connection, more long-lasting partnerships with a zeal for reciprocity. Thanks, Dave. This talkative kid from Chinatown is now a fifty-two-year-old woman who is on a mission.

I would like to express my deepest gratitude to the executives, colleagues, and customers who took the time to be interviewed about their CAB experiences. These people are invaluable beyond measure and bring the book to life. Your willingness to share your time, insights, and expertise has not only shaped this book, but has also enriched this field.

This book would not have been possible without your heartfelt contributions: Adam, Yoav, Tamir, Josh, Jerry, Denis, Vikram, Randy, Anita, Naveed, Gareth, Karl, Jace, and Jason. Your voices, stories, anecdotes, and perspectives from your CAB experiences have enhanced the book with a warmth and authenticity that I am truly grateful for. It is your voices and experiences that have given life to the concepts and ideas within these pages.

To Yoav, my walking buddy, who allowed me to endlessly ramble about the CAB ideas on trails. Yoav, remember our meeting-up that fall night, when I was about to give up? We probably walked three miles in circles, and you didn't let me give up.

Extra gratitude to Michael, Alan, Steve, Monique, Siobhan, Kim, Josh, Wei, Anita A, Anita R, Lori, Dave, Taka, Stephanie, Carmen, and Karyn for being my early beta readers. I am humbled by your dedication and commitment to support me during the tender "review" stage. Your involvement has shown that you are not just advisers, but the sincerest CAB on my new journey. Your willingness to be just a phone call away for discussions, clarifications, and further exploration has been a testament to "you"!

To Josh, I have so much gratitude for your time and willingness to talk more. Our time on the phone gave me an extra boost to help me complete this book with ease.

To Alan, thank you for being my mentor, for teaching me how to fish. Your twenty-three-plus years of generosity—mentoring me, being willing to take quick calls to bounce ideas around, giving me not just work guidance but personal coaching—has always come from your heart. Thank you especially for taking me under your wing with no marketing experience and sending me off to Storage Networking World, first to fix up our new modern pop-up 10 by 10-foot booth, which still took me two hours, is something I'll always chuckle about and cherish. I was so glad to see you the next day, you said after inspecting the booth, "Nice work!"

To Anita, I'm grateful you were my manager at RingCentral. My later and memorable career experiences are being led by you. I was in awe at every challenge you took on. Thank you for especially mentoring me in the later part of my life. You're a compass with heart and intention, guiding me and coaching me during my new journey.

To Shannon, my sister and coach, you have the biggest, most generous heart. Every call we have, I walk away lifted. Thank you for more than twenty years of coaching.

To Hilary, you've been a constant and guiding star for me. You've helped me grow and reflect and question every step of the way. Thank you for always reminding me of positivity, advising me to take more time to celebrate, and encouraging me to write this book.

To Ryan, for truly letting me be vulnerable and getting me prepared to put myself out there. And for being my cube buddy and always being willing to support me.

To Andy, just when I was going to give up on finding a designer, you appeared. Thank you for giving me the perfect book cover design, for being a top-notch human being, and for being a kick-ass designer!

To Kristen, who worked day in and day out for a steady three-plus months to help me rewrite the manuscript. I was really down when I started to rewrite, and your daily edits and feedback kept me going to find my voice and write. I'm forever grateful for your time, encouragement, and hard work.

To Siobhan, I am so grateful for your review of my final manuscript. You know my voice so well. You're amazing.

To Julia, thanks for giving my book structure and flow, but also sharing that all the hard work paid off with Kristen. Thanks for also answering all my newbie questions about publishing.

To Terry, I am eternally grateful that you picked up the phone and put on your cape to save me not once, but twice. Thank you for helping with edits and the book layout when another editor didn't want to. You've got this huge heart, Terry. Thanks!

To Rebecca, for taking on the manuscript while also juggling so much and introducing me to Emily. I appreciate all the detailed edits you made during my final journey.

To Emily, for jumping in and explaining the edits with clarity, and making it easy to read through the final manuscript. Although this is your first time proofing, you hit it out of the park!

To Lori, for being a world-class publicist, giving me more advice even before I signed and access to your impressive network. You're the best at representation and have high integrity. Thank you for building up my business and book.

My dearest Auntie Lea, and Karen, who've been supportive of writing this book when I was down. Gail, thanks for your advice early on to keep me on track and focused. Your support and love mean so much, not just now, but through all the losses. I don't think I even heard an "aiyaaaa" when I decided to retire early, write a book, and become a consultant.

To Milou and Mia, always beside me, reminding me to take breaks. Milou, I miss you every day and thank you for leading me to Mia. Your unconditional love fills my heart and soul.

To Clyde, this book is dedicated to you, my family, my best friend. It couldn't have happened without you guiding me. Thank you for being my light.

Thank you all for being the heartbeat of this project, and for sharing your warmth, wisdom, and guidance.

With sincerity,

Irene

www.ingramcontent.com/pod-product-compliance
Lightning Source LLC
La Vergne TN
LVHW012012240125
801961LV00034B/507